The
Plant Doctor

By Richard Nicholls

Illustrated by Edwina McFarlane

This book may be ordered directly from the publisher.
Please include 25¢ postage.
Try your bookstore first.

Running Press, 38 South Nineteenth Street,
Philadelphia, Pennsylvania 19103

Printed in the United States of America
Distributed in Canada by Van Nostrand Reinhold Ltd., Ontario
Library of Congress Catalog Card Number 74-31542
ISBN 0-914294-14-8

Art direction and Design by Jim Wilson with Tom Fetterman
Cover Art and interior illustrations by Edwina McFarlane
Our thanks to the Pennsylvania Horticultural Society for their advice
and kind assistance
Type: Optima, Composition by Alpha Publications, Inc.
Cover printed by Pearl Pressman Liberty
The Plant Doctor printed and bound by Port City Press

Fourth printing, February 1976

The Plant Doctor

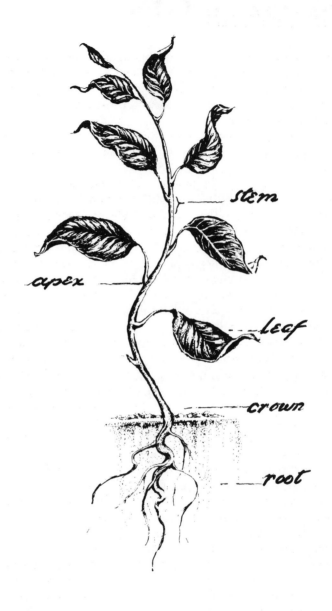

stem

apex

leaf

crown

root

major parts of plant

First Words

Civilization can sometimes be measured as society's pursuit of progress. And if progress can be defined as advanced technology, high density of population, increased standard of living and the partial control of nature itself, then progress we have—in abundance—*in excess*.

In fact, progress means that many kids in today's high rise, unisex, television and supermarket culture have never seen a live cow, tree or forest.

In fact, progress means that America's great outdoors is shrinking; every day almost 2,000 acres fall to the dreaded sub-dividers.

Many young people are concerned with society's apparent cavalier attitude towards nature. The ecology movement was a direct response to it. Also, I believe, today's plant boom is a reflection of—a reaction against—the ungreening of America. If we must live in concrete and glass cities, at least let us have plants in abundance to remind us of what we compromised in exchange for progress.

I preface this book with a few personal opinions and observations in order to explain what plants mean to me, and, perhaps, you as well. I assume that you already have plants or else you wouldn't have bought this book. And if you have plants, you *will* eventually have problems. No, you will not be lucky and escape problems by religiously watering and sunning your plants. Nor will your green thumb or your ability to telepathically communicate with your plants help you avoid the problems that will inevitably come.

The Plant Doctor is a guide to green health. It will, I hope, help you to avoid many common and uncommon plant problems through regular care and preventative maintenance. But it will also help you bring your ailing plants back to health once they begin to fail by explaining the symptoms, underlying causes and cures for all the troubles commonly afflicting house plants.

I think that a brief word on Chapter 2 is in order. Chapter 2 is perhaps the most important section of the entire book because it lists for quick reference all the major plant symptoms and their possible causes. Each listing in the guide is keyed to an appropriate page or chapter reference. While every problem covered in the book is mentioned in Chapter 2, I urge you, of course, to read **The Plant Doctor** from cover to cover at least once in order to better understand the function of your plant and the nature of their problems.

Good luck!

Chapter 1
The Patients

foliage

flowering

Most house plants belong to one of three major groupings.

Foliage house plants are distinguished by the multitude of shapes and sizes their leaves assume. While some foliage plants do flower, their blooms are only occasional, and it is the foliage itself that makes this large group of plants so attractive. In addition, many foliage plants are especially hardy and adaptable.

Flowering house plants regularly produce colorful and often quite exotic flowers. Many types will bloom year after year. Flowering plants are somewhat sensitive to the environment and require more care than other types of plants.

7

succulents

cacti

Cacti and succulents compose the third major group. These plants feature unusual and often quite startling forms. Some types produce blooms that are beautiful, but all too brief. Cacti and succulents generally require more sunlight—and less water—than either foliage or flowering house plants. In addition, most cacti will adapt without damage to an environment having little humidity.

There are also several minor sub-groupings, such as ferns and gesneriads, but since each sub-grouping is an exception in itself, there are no general descriptions that would be applicable.

SHOPPING FOR HOUSEPLANTS

Buy your house plants from people who *know* house plants. Don't buy expensive plants at a variety shop, supermarket or department store—purchase your plants from professional people who grow and sell plants, and nothing else. They usually know the most about house plants, and are both able and willing to answer your questions.

8

After all, their success depends on the reputation they build; if a department store runs a shoddy plant shop, the store will survive even if the plant department does not. But a plant store that acquires a reputation for selling diseased or infested plants, price gouging or shoddy service has nothing else to sell to carry it through, and will soon fail.

So if you are serious about building a plant collection, buy the more expensive or rare plants *only* at a plant shop. I know many people regularly buy plants from florists, but I hesitate to recommend them. Florists sell cut and arranged flowers. House plants are usually only a side line, and I admit to the suspicion that many florists know little and care less about house plants, judging by the misinformed advice I have received from several florists. But, if there are no plant stores in your area, florists are a preferable source to most other suppliers.

No matter where you shop for a plant, and no matter whether you intend to spend $1 or $100, always take a long, close look at the plant that interests you. Do the leaves have a healthy green color? Are there any holes in the leaves, or do they have ravelled edges? Are there leaves conspicuosly missing?

Do you notice any symptoms of an insect infestation, such as webs or damage to the stems or leaves? You might even want to lift up several leaves to examine the undersides for indications of bugs.

Are there any white growths on the soil surface or on leaves? Is the plant wilted, listless and bent, or does it stand straight up? What sort of a guarantee, if any, does the store offer with its plants?

Don't just go in and buy a plant. Look around—if the shop appears dirty, ill ventilated and the plants appear crammed together, you would do well to look elsewhere.

But let's say you've found a good shop, stocked with healthy plants and run by knowledgeable, helpful sales people. You've settled on a plant that will not only meet your budget, but adapt to the amount of light available in your home. Remember—don't throw your money away: buy only those plants that can adapt to the conditions prevailing in your home. Don't buy plants by their looks alone—buy them because you can grow them by giving them what they need. So you've found the ideal plant—now how do you get it home?

You get them home *very carefully*. Ask to have the plant wrapped in plastic or paper. Try not to carry a plant around with you—take it directly home. During the winter, I recommend that you buy only the hardiest of plants. Taking a tender tropical or fragile fern out into wintry weather will probably throw it into trauma, no matter how carefully you protect it.

When you get a plant home, don't immediately plunk it down with your other plants. Isolate it for at least a week. Clean its leaves, water it and watch it. If the plant goes into shock—that is, if it wilts, pales or sheds leaves or flowers—examine it for disease by turning it out, inspecting the roots, and carefully searching the plant for mushy, decayed tissue. Check the soil and plant for insects. If you cannot find evidence of infection or infestation, the plant is suffering from trauma. That is, it has found it difficult to adapt to the temperature and light conditions in your house. Enclose the plant in a plastic bag, mist it, seal the bag and watch it carefully for two to three days. Open the bag once or twice a day, for fifteen minutes at a time, or punch several small holes in the bag in order to allow air to circulate. Such treatment should be sufficient to bring the plant round. Move it gradually into its permanent position, being careful not to move it immediately into direct sunlight.

And if something goes wrong, and you feel you are not at fault, *complain*. You may not get a refund, but you might get another plant. The house plant market has grown remarkably fast—in some cases outdistancing fair business practices. If you shop carefully, compare prices and inspect potential purchases carefully, you can avoid becoming a victim.

Use caution if you purchase plants or bulbs through the mail. Buy only from established houses offering a guarantee on their merchandise.

If you use your native good sense, you need not come out the loser when you buy plants.

PLANT WORK AREA

It's a good idea to establish some portion of your rooms as a plant work area. A folding card table will be sufficient for all but the largest of indoor plant collections. One or two shelves will also prove quite useful. Use this area to store your supplies of fertilizer, soil and chemicals, as well as your tools. Do your transplantings, pottings and prunings on the table, where you will have enough room to work without being cramped. In addition, the area can become your operating table and recovery room for diseased or infected plants.

You must keep this working area scrupulously clean. Discard used soil and dead foliage as soon as you work is done, and regularly scrub the table with a cleanser to remove the possibility of infections. If you have extra pots sitting about, scrub them out. Keep all the containers of plant food or chemicals closed and out of the sunlight. I have found coffee cans to be just the right size for holding extra amounts of a soil mix or various soil components. But remember to keep anything questionable clearly labeled.

10

You may also want to keep some part of this area, or a space nearby, as an isolation ward for new plants, or for infected plants that you are treating. Such an area should receive plenty of indirect light and be protected from drafts.

What tools do you need for proper plant care?

First of all, you need a long-spouted watering can.

You also definitely need a plastic spray bottle, to apply a fine mist of water onto your plants. You might want to have two spray bottles—one for water and one for the application of chemicals.

You will need several small tools, including a hand rake, to stir or loosen soil; you will also need a trowel, to shovel soil up.

You will need a sharp hand knife, or a razor, to take cuttings or remove dead tissue—and you should have a supply of denatured alcohol to keep the knife clean.

You should have a supply of labels, to identify plants and containers in your work area. A bundle of small sticks, to prop up plant parts, may be also prove helpful.

Keep a sheet of plastic, or several large plastic bags on hand, for use as an emergency recovery room. In fact, if you have a number of plants, you may want to clean out an unused aquarium for use as an emergency room. Then, when you are faced with a traumatized plant, you can put it inside the aquarium (provided the unit is of sufficient height), and simply cover the top with plastic. If the aquarium is not tall enough, you might try standing it up on its end and taping the cover to the side.

You should have a soil test kit and a hygrometer on hand. And you may find that a sturdy thermometer will be of some use in determining temperature levels in various parts of your house.

And I've found it very practical to keep an apron nearby. Transplanting, potting and some other operations can end up graphically recorded on your clothes.

I have found it handy and time-saving to keep a supply of several sizes of pots on hand, as well as crockery or window screening. The fewer trips you have to make to gather materials for a plant session, the better.

It is vitally important to keep your working area constantly clean and in order. It will speed and simplify your work, and greatly reduce the risk of infections spreading once you have removed a plant from its normal spot. An infection or a pest can be spread to several plants by a dirty tool. And you can expect pests to seek haven wherever there is a pile of decaying organic material or a pile of uncleaned pots. Your working area is your operating room—now what would *you* think of a doctor who worked in a dirty operating room?

The first requirement of a plant doctor is cleanliness. And the second is order. With such qualities, you can decrease problems among your plants and often greatly increase their health and longevity.

12

Chapter 2
The Problems

yellowed & browned leaves

A comprehensive list of the symptoms of plant problems would require a book at least the size of this present volume. And you really do not need such a detailed listing unless you intend to make plant doctoring your career. I have, therefore, made a simplified list of the most commonly occuring major plant symptoms.

Under each major symptom, all of the possible causes of the problem are listed and page references to the text are given. So if you have a plant with, for example, yellowing leaves, you may have to check six or seven possibilities in the text before you identify the problem. It may sound tedious, but this method should produce a positive identification of the problem. In addition, your checking should enlighten you about other potential problems in time to correct them.

To best assist your ailing plants, I suggest that you read the entire book from cover to cover. After you have a general knowledge of causes and cures, consult this chapter for specific problems and emergencies. Every problem discussed in **The Plant Doctor** is listed in this chapter.

A. LEAVES
I. Leaves become discolored, yellow or browned when:

CAUSE	REFERENCE IN TEXT
1. A plant outgrows its pot.	19
2. The soil is over-alkaline.	29
3. There is a nitrogen deficiency.	30
4. There is a phosphorus deficiency.	31
(Leaves turn a brighten green, then purple, finally becoming mottled.)	
5. There is a magnesium deficiency.	31
(Leaves brown in the center while remaining green along the margins, or while they whiten on the margins.)	
6. There is an inadequate supply of light.	36
7. Watering is too infrequent.	40
8. There is insufficient humidity.	45
(Leaves turn brown at the tip, while yellowing along the margins.)	

THE PLANT DOCTOR

VI. Leaves fall off the plant because:
1. There is a deficiency of nitrogen. 30
2. There is an insufficient supply of potassium. 31
3. There is a deficiency of magnesium. 31
4. There is too little humidity. 45
5. Temperatures are too high, or too low. 50, 51
6. The plant is reacting to gas or smoke. 54
7. The plant has been insufficiently watered. 40
8. The plant is not getting a proper amount of light. 36
9. The plant is under attack by some disease, such as leaf spot or mildew. 86, 87
10. The plant is being attacked by insects. 58, 59

VII. Leaves exhibit tip burns because of:
1. A potassium deficiency. 31
2. A lack of humidity in the environment. 45
3. Smoke or pollution damage. 54
4. Overwatering. 40
   (Leaf tips become brittle, while scabby bubbles appear on the underside.)
5. An anthracnose infection, in which the tips turn brown while brown depressions appear on the leaves. 83
6. An attack of chlorosis, turning tips brown or white. 84
7. An exposure to too much sunlight. 36

VIII. Defoliation of a plant is caused by:
1. Insufficient potassium. 31
   (plant defoliates from the base upwards.) 31
2. A magnesium deficency. 50, 51
3. Temperatures either too high or too low. 54
4. Smoke or gas damage. 36
5. An inadequate supply of light. 36
   (defoliation occurs from the base upwards.)
6. An inadequate supply of water. 40
7. An insect attack. 57

A   **IX.** Holes appear in leaves because of an insect attack.
1. Gaping, ragged holes are caused by: 61
   . . .caterpillars 63
   . . .cockroaches 64
   . . .cutworms 73
   . . .or snails, slugs. 63
2. Holes chewed in young, tender foliage are caused by crickets. 76, 77
3. Small, round holes in leaves are chewed by springtails. 65, 66
4. Holes appearing in leaves and flowers can be caused by foliage insects, such as earwigs. 67, 68
5. Irregular tunnels appearing between leaf surfaces indicate leafminers. 64
6. Flower heads slashed through, or stems snapped off, are the work of cutworms. 61, 62
7. Leaves speckled with black excrement indicates the presence of caterpillars   . . .or leafminers. 67, 68

CAUSE	REFERENCE IN TEXT

B. A plant's growth rate slows far down or stops, indicating that:

1. It is potbound and should be transplanted.	**19**
2. It is suffering from a deficiency of nutrients.	**30, 31**
3. It is receiving inadequate light.	**36**
4. Temperatures are too high or too low.	**50, 51**
5. It has been damaged by pollution.	**54**
6. It is suffering from chlorosis.	**84**
7. It has been damaged by an infection, or an attack of some plant pest.	**57**
8. It is crammed too closely against other plants.	**84**

C. Soil.

If soil crumbles away from the sides of a pot, it may be because:

1. The plant has become potbound, and roots are displacing soil.	**19**
2. The plant has been drastically underwatered.	**40**
A white crust coating the soil surface is caused by a build-up of fertilizer salts.	**34**
A pasty white or grayish mold appears on the soil surface because of overwatering.	**87**
Soil producing bubbles of water when it is probed indicates chronic overwatering or poor drainage.	**40, 21**

D. Types of rots include:

1. Crown and Stem Rot, in which the crown and stems turn soft and mushy.	**85**
2. Root rot, which causes roots to turn soft and mushy. Plants fail because the root system can no longer perform its many tasks.	**88**
3. Roots become sufficiently damaged to admit a rot infection because they have been:	**20, 22, 25**
—Handled too roughly during the potting procedure.	**21**
—Given poor drainage, and as they constantly sit in wet soil.	**40**
—Consistently overwatered.	**57**
—Disturbed, damaged or weakened by the attacks of movements of pests.	

E. Insects attacking roots include:

1. Symphylans (Garden Centipedes), which gnaw young roots and root hairs. Roots look gnawed and misshapen.	**62**
2. Fungus Gnats, which attack root hairs and chew root tissue. Small roots vanish while large roots become badly scarred.	**66, 67**
3. Millipedes, which feed on small roots or root hairs.	**70**
4. Nematodes, which attack roots, causing galls and knots to appear on roots while the roots become distorted and die.	**71**
5. Snowbug, which feeds on small roots.	**74**
6. Springtails, which chew small round holes in new roots.	**76, 77**

F. Flower buds and flowers.
  1. Blasted buds (buds fall off without opening) can be caused by:
    . . .insufficient calcium — 31
    . . .mites — 75, 76
    . . .thrips — 77
    . . .or white fly. — 78
  2. Buds opening only part-way, and producing withered blooms, can be caused by:
    . . .inadequate light — 36
    . . .inadequate water — 40
    . . .or inadequate humidity. — 45
  3. Buds shriveling and dropping off are caused by a lack of humidity.
  4. Deformed flowers indicate:
    . . .an attack of thrips — 77
    . . .or insufficient nutrients. — 31
  5. Colorless, limp flowers indicate a lack of light. — 36

G. Stems
  1. Stems rot because of overwatering. — 40
  2. Stems appear weak because of:
    . . .an overdose of nitrogen — 30
    . . .insufficient nutrients — 31
    . . .or insufficient water. — 40
  3. Insects that attack stems include:
    sowbugs, which chew stems. — 74
    aphidis, which cause them to become weak, attenuated. — 60, 61
    cutworms, which may slash stems off. — 64
    symphylans, which gnaw the submerged portion of a stem. — 62

H. If you have pets, suspect their activity if you find:
  1. Plants with a compacted soil surface. — 55
  2. Holes dug into the soil. — 55
  3. Smashed pots. — 55
  4. Torn foliage, snapped stems or chewed leaves or flowers. — 55

I. While specific insects are mentioned above, I consider it necessary to provide a brief listing of the damage each type of plant pest can cause. If the damage seems to describe one of your suffering plants, try to locate the insect and consult the pages indicated by the column on the right.
  1. **Aphids**–are small, soft, green-bodied insects that cause leaves to curl and pucker, stems to weaken and droop. Tiny white dots on leaves could be dead aphids. — 60, 61
  2. **Caterpillars** are wormlike creatures, may be quite large, and come in a variety of colors. They leave black specks of excrement on leaves and tear gaping holes in leaves overnight. They also will devour whole leaves. — 61, 62

3. Symphylans (*Garden Centipedes*) *have white, flattened, wormlike* **62**
    bodies. They gnaw on young roots and root hairs, and the
    submerged section of the plant's stem.
4. Cockroaches *are familiar household pests that sometimes tear and* **63**
    chew chunks out of plant leaves and flowers.
5. Crickets *chew away tender new leaves.* **63**
6. Cutworms *have large, soft, smooth, wormlike bodies. They slash* **64**
    through the stems of seedlings and young plants, slash stems and
    flowers away from plants, and sometimes tear large, irregular
    chunks out of leaves, working inwards from the margins.
7. Earthworms *have a wormlike appearence, and they may disturb the* **65**
    roots by creating many tunnels.
8. Earwigs *are dark brown beetle-like insects about an inch long. They* **65, 66**
    chew holes in leaves and flowers.
9. Fungus Gnats *are the gray or sooty black dots that hover over plant* **66, 67**
    foliage. Their eggs hatch on the soil; the maggots burrow down
    and feed on root tissue and root hairs. Root rot and other
    diseases often follow on attack.
10. Leafminers *create a characteristic "mined" effect on leaf surfaces.* **67, 68**
    Leaves appear speckled with excrement, may shrivel, and may
    turn yellow or brown or become blistered.
11. Leafrollers *are small caterpillars that roll themselves up into leaves.* **68**
    Leaves die and plant growth wilts as a result of their attack.
12. Mealybugs *appear as white powdery masses clinging to leaf axils or* **69**
    stem joints. Their attack will defoliate or badly wilt a plant.
13. Millipedes *are hard-shelled insects with a cylindrical body. They feed* **70**
    on new roots and slash through the stems of seedlings.
14. Nematodes *are microscopic creatures that cause roots to develop galls* **71**
    or knots, or to become shrunken and distorted. Leaves wilt,
    growth ceases and the plant may die.
15. Scale *appear as brown discs attached to the surfaces of plant parts.* **72**
    Leaves become spotted or mottled, turn yellow and fall off.
16. Snails and Slugs *chew rough holes through leaves and drop a slimy* **73**
    trail as they travel.
17. Sowbugs *have a brown flat oval bodies and feed on young roots,* **74**
    stems and seedlings. Foliage pales, and some stems may be
    chewed right off the plant.
18. Spider Mites *are so tiny as to be almost invisible. They spin coarse* **75, 76**
    webbing across leaf axils or between leaves. An infested plant
    develops mottled leaves having gray and green splotches, and
    the plant may defoliate.
19. Springtails *have round, dark, soft bodies with yellow markings. They* **76, 77**
    chew small round holes in leaves, young roots or seedlings.
20. Thrips *are tiny needle-like insects that scar leaves, causing pockmarks* **77**
    and whitened surfaces on the underside of leaves. Flower buds
    drop off, and leaves acquire a papery texture and develop
    blisters.
21. White flies *are small, white moth-like pests that cause leaves to* **78**
    yellow, wilt and fall off. They excrete a sticky substance that
    forms a medium for the growth of molds.

Chapter 3

Plants and Pots

Most house plants eventually outgrow their pots. It may take two or three years, but it will happen. And when it does, don't take it as a calamity. Repotting a plant is a simple, brief operation—just consider the problem a compliment to your plants skills. (Repotting is the term generally used to indicate maintaining a plant in the same-sized pot by trimming back the plant's roots. Potting-on refers to the process of transferring a plant into a larger container.) You've given a plant what is needs, kept it healthy, and it has responded by doing what it's supposed to do—grow.

A plant that has grown uncomfortable in its container will begin growing at a noticeably slower rate. Older foliage may yellow, while new foliage may grow in discolored and distorted, or may even remain green and healthy while the rest of the plant wilts and fades. The soil of such a plant will be constantly dry, no matter how often it is watered. The roots of the plant may push upwards through the soil surface or probe downwards through the drainage hole, resembling tentative, knotty fingers.

If you suspect a plant is potbound, turn it out for an examination. To do this, place one hand over the soil surface, positioning the plant stem securely between two fingers. Grasp the base of the pot with your other hand. Invert the pot, and then pull the plant free by gently tugging the pot away. If the plant remains wedged in the pot, tap the container carefully against a hard surface. Then if the plant and its root ball *still* will not slide out, run a dull knife around the interior of the pot along the sides.

When you have removed the plant from the pot, set the plant gently on a clean work surface. A pot-bound plant will have a dense, tangled mass of roots. Proliferating roots displace soil, gradually

19

pushing the soil out through the drainage holes. And less soil means less water retention. The less water available to a plant, the more it will yellow and wilt. Struggling to survive, a plant may allocate more of its diminished water supply to some portion of its growth, while neglecting other parts. That means that new growth may thrive while mature growth wilts or drops off. Or it may be just the opposite. Plants often respond to illness by shedding non-vital parts such as leaves, buds and flowers.

You may want to hold a plant at its present size because you don't want your efficiency apartment to become a tropical jungle. If so, you can trim the roots and report the plant in the same or a similarly-sized pot. Or, if you want the plant to continue to expand, you can pot it in the next largest size container.

If you intend to repot a plant, turn it out and clean away all of the soil clinging to its roots. Use your hands to gently brush away large clots of soil, then hold the roots under a mild flow of lukewarm water to rinse off any remainder. Handle the roots carefully, for they can be easily bruised or damaged. Cut overly-long roots back far enough for them to fit comfortably in the pot. Make certain to cut the roots along their joints. If any roots have become damaged or diseased because of overcrowding, cut them off at their point of origin.

You should repot as soon as you are finished pruning the roots. Be sure to keep the roots moist the entire time they are exposed. The moisture they receive while you are rinsing them off should be sufficient, but if your work is interrupted, rinse the roots again and enclose the entire root ball in a plastic bag.

To repot the plant, follow the procedure for potting given below. Mist the repotted plant several times each day for at least a week. If the plant exhibits symptoms of trauma, enclose the entire plant in a plastic bag, but be certain to give the plant a good watering before you settle it in the bag. Then tie the bag shut, and punch several ½" air holes in the sides of the bag. Leave the plant alone in its miniature oxygen tent until it appears to have recuperated.

Move up only one pot size when you transplant. Never, *never* jump ahead by several pot sizes in the hope of postponing your next potting session. A plant potted in an over-large container will keel over. Or worse, the soil may become waterlogged, as the plant just will not need the supply of water the container can hold. Worst of all, the roots may become damaged, and a rot may settle in. So please, take it a size at a time?

You want to pot-on, but into what? Many different types of containers are available. There are clay pots and plastic pots, hanging baskets and decorative containers—whatever your requirements of space and shape, there will be a container to fulfill it.

20

The most commonly used—and recognizable—of containers are the standard and azalea pots. Standard pots have a depth equal to their width (measured across the rim of a pot.) Azalea pots have a depth three-quarters of their width. Standard pots are round, while azalea pots are available in either round or square shapes. Both standard and azalea pots are manufactured in sizes that increase an inch at a time. So if your plant has outgrown a 4" azalea pot, you should be shopping for a 5" azalea pot.

Most house plants do well in standard pots. Cane, rhizomatous and semperflorens begonias prefer azalea pots, as do bromeliads, cacti, African violets and, yes, azaleas.

You settle on a standard pot. But of what material should it be made? At the local garden center, you will find a bewildering array of standard pots made of clay, hard and soft plastic pots, ceramic pots, decorated pots and metal pots. Clay and hard plastic pots are the most versatile and popular materials. Never, *never* use a soft plastic pot for house plants.

Either clay or plastic pots may be used. Some of the variables you might consider in your choice should include the facts that:

Clay Pots
—Are available in one color, the familiar earthy red.

—Are more fragile than plastic.
—Allow water to evaporate through their porous walls, so that plants are evenly watered.

—Are heavier, and thus well suited to balancing top heavy plants.
—Leach damaging fertilizer salts out of the soil.
—Provide even, rapid absorption of water.

Plastic Pots
—Are available in a wide range of colors.
—Are usually less expensive.

—Allow water to evaporate only from the surface. Moisture is thus retained longer, which is beneficial to plants requiring constant moisture.
—Are lighter, and thus easier to move.

—Maintain constant moisture for a long period of time.

Unless you have particular needs in decorating a room, I suggest you choose either a clay or plastic pot. But never buy any pot unless it has a drainage hole (or holes.) The holes allow excess water to drain out of a plant's soil after a watering. And they help aerate the roots. Without drainage, the soil may become waterlogged. Sodden soil encourages the growth and diffusion of rots or fungus infections.

21

Soil can also become compacted around roots, smothering them. If the pot you're admiring doesn't have drainage holes, put it down and pick up one that does have holes. That holeless pot may be pretty, but I assure you that your plant will face extra problems that you and it don't need.

Having said that, I must qualify that advice. You may find that plants you purchased from some shop have been potted in containers without drainage holes, and they've been doing fine. Some distributors do pot plants in closed containers, but they sidestep the potential problem by adding a thick layer of perlite, charcoal or gravel. You can do the same thing if you absolutely intend to put a plant in a pot having no drainage holes. I don't recommend it for small plants, but for very large plants, it is often the only practical method.

POTTING LARGE PLANTS

Large plants are difficult to transplant because of their weight and bulk. If you have a green giant that needs repotting or potting-on, recruit a friend (or friends) to help out.

First give the plant a good watering. Grasp it by the lower portion of its stem and lift it out of the pot. Meanwhile, your friend (or friends) should tug the pot off.

If you have run out of room for the plant to expand, pot the plant in its old container after removing as much of the old soil as you can. Use fresh pasteurized soil, pouring it in around the stem until it has reached the soil line. Then gently push the soil downwards with your palms, but do not lean heavily on the soil. Too much pressure will compact the soil around the root. It is especially important that the stem is entirely upright.

Follow the same procedure for potting-on.

When the rootball of the large plant refuses to crumble away, take a clean, sharp knife and make several vertical incisions in the rootball. This will loosen the soil

and encourage the growth of new roots. However, it can also disrupt roots and introduce rot, so use this procedure only when the ball of soil will not yield to other methods.

It is impractical to pot very large plants in containers having drainage holes. You probably will not be able to find a saucer large enough to sit beneath a big pot, and without some receptacle to catch the water, you will have constant moisture around and under the pot.

You can place a large potted plant inside a yet larger container. The container should have an inch of gravel charcoal or perlite lining its bottom. Put the plant on top of the gravel, so that it will sit well out of any water run-off. Empty the container once every several months.

Or, you can put an inch or more of perlite in the bottom of a large plant's pot. But *water very sparingly*. I've seen this done and have had assurances from others of its success, but I hesitate to recommend this procedure. Use it only if your ingenuity fails you.

Hand-crafted clay pots and decorative containers generally have no drainage holes. You can use an electric drill to make several small holes, and then put the re-conditioned pot on a saucer. Or you can hide a clay or plastic pot within a decorative pot large enough to camouflage the proletarian pot. Put a layer of gravel in the decorative container so that the inner pot will not sit in water. Every month, lift the plant out and pour off any water that has collected in the bottom of the larger container.

Each pot must sit on a saucer, which catches the water that runs out of the pot. It should be emptied a half-hour after each watering. Plastic saucers are available in a wide range of sizes and colors.

So you decide on a pot, and you take it home. Wash it thoroughly in warm soapy water, then rinse it. If you intend to re-use a pot, soak it in a solution composed of nine parts warm water to one part household bleach. After allowing the pot to soak, remove it and rinse it once, then again to flush away any traces of bleach. If there are accumulations of white fertilizer salts or other growths on a pot's walls, scrub the pot with a stiff-bristled brush after it has soaked.

Keep a clay pot in a container of lukewarm water until you are ready to pot. That is because a dry clay pot will thirstily soak up most of the water you give your just-potted plant, depriving it of vital nourishment.

You're ready to pot. You've cleared away a work area. The just-washed pot is before you. What else do you need?

You need crockery—perhaps shards from a broken clay pot or some other coarse material. The material must be concave, as it must be placed in an arch over a pot's drainage holes. This material prevents soil from filtering out of the pot, or from being carried out in

23

larger amounts with each watering. Some gardeners I've heard of use window screening positioned over the drainage holes instead of crockery. The screening is then covered with a layer of perlite to prevent any soil from sifting through, while allowing water to percolate through. Either material is acceptable, as long as you wash it thoroughly before using it. Position the material so that it covers—but does not block—the drainage holes. If crockery is pressed directly against the holes, no water will pass through, and damage will result.

If a newly-potted plant wilts while its soil is constantly soaked with water, the drainage material is obstructing the water flow; the soil is becoming waterlogged, and the plant is in danger of suffering real damage. Turn the plant out and rearrange the drainage material.

So you have positioned the material over the drainage holes. Your soil mix has been prepared, and you have it at hand. Pour enough of the soil (or perlite, if you are using screening over the drainage holes) into the pot to thoroughly cover the drainage material.

Now turn the plant out. Quickly inspect the roots for signs of damage or disease, and prune any damaged or diseased roots back to their healthy parts. Brush away the old soil, and rinse the soil off the roots of diseased or infested plants with a gentle spray of lukewarm water. Do not, however, attempt to clean the soil from the roots of cacti or avocado plants, as they have extremely tender roots. In such cases, brush off as much of the old soil as you can, and then directly pot the plant.

Stand the plant in the pot so that its roots spread out and rest on the soil surface. The old soil line should appear as the cessation of dark tissue on the plant's crown, and the tissue above it will be much lighter. The line should be ½" to ¾" below the rim of the pot. Add or subtract soil until you are satisfied that the line is properly established

in relation to the pot's rim. Pour the soil in over the roots and up around the plant with a slow, regular motion. *Don't* just dump the soil in. Lift the pot after pouring some soil in, and tap the pot against a hard surface. Add soil, and repeat the tapping. This should settle the soil and eliminate any air pockets. If the pot is too large or unwieldy to admit such treatment, press the soil down by applying an even pressure with your fingers. Be firm, but don't bring all of your weight to bear, as you might compact the soil or damage the roots. As you work, study the plant to be certain that it is upright, and not leaning or wobbly. If it is not straight, growth can be hampered.

Bring the soil up to the old soil line—no more and no less. When you are finished, water the plant. Also, fill in any gaps that appear in the soil. Then check to be sure the water is draining from the plant without obstruction.

Give the plant a location with plenty of indirect light and good ventilation. Be sure to keep the plant out of direct sunlight for an entire day. Also mist the leaves several times. As long as the plant shows no signs of trauma, you may return it to its usual location and watering and feeding schedule the following day.

Wilting on a just-potted plant is a sure sign of trauma. Soft-leaved plants seem most sensitive to transfer trauma. If wilting does occur, spray the plant's leaves with lukewarm water and encase the plant in a plastic bag. Twist the bag closed, punch one or two air holes, and allow the plant to recuperate in its protected environment for two or three days.

SEEDLINGS

Be *very* careful when you pot seedlings. Their small, soft parts are especially vulnerable to damage. Use small pots for seedlings. Fill a pot with your soil mix, then take any slim, sharp-tipped object and make a small hole in the center of the soil surface. Use a spoon to lift a seedling out of its old environment and into its pot. Gently grasp the seedling by a leaf and settle it into the hole. Make certain not to touch the seedling's roots and stem. Holding it upright, tap the soil in around it. Be sure that the seedling can stand upright, and that the roots are entirely covered. Water it, and give it a well ventilated, indirectly illuminated spot. If the seedling does not seem to be adjusting well to its new container, water it and put it—pot and all—into a small plastic bag. Twist the bag closed and leave the seedling inside until it shows signs of recovery.

CACTI

Cacti prove the exception to potting procedures. Cacti should be repotted no more than once every two years, and then only if they exhibit signs of cramping. Use a clay pot, as clay will evaporate moisture more rapidly.

Be very careful not to bruise the roots when you are transferring a cactus. Its roots are easily damaged as well as easily infected. Be certain that the plant retains the old soil line—if too much is exposed, a plant can become lopsided. If too little stem is exposed, and the old line covered over, rot will result. After potting, give the cactus *no water* for the first two weeks in its new container. And, contrary to other house plants, put it into direct sunlight as soon as the transfer is completed.

Chapter 4
Plants and Soil

Never pot a plant in unpasteurized soil.
Never.

Unpasteurized soil is the soil you walk on. It is the soil in your back yard, or the earth in some local park. It *may* contain some of the nutrients a house plant requires. It certainly *will* contain a wide assortment of the things a house plant definitely does not need, including insect eggs or larva, disease spores, bacteria, animal wastes and other nameless effluvia. Don't use it.

Buy pasteurized soil at a plant shop or garden supply center. Pasteurized soil has been cleansed of harmful impurities. It is available as a prepacked soil mix, or as isolated soil components, which you can buy and combine for your own soil formula.

Yes, the soil all around you doesn't cost you anything. But it will cost you when you lose a plant to a disease or pest *you* introduced through the soil. And pasteurized soil doesn't cost all that much. If you have a modest collection of plants, you will need to spend very little money on soil. Plants just don't require potting that often. And if you have a large plant collection, you can purchase pasteurized soil components in large, bargain-priced sizes.

Soil is the anchor of almost all green life. But it is not, as we assume, just "dirt"—a brown homogenous substance. It is in fact a loose and constantly altering collection of organic and mineral substances in varying stages of decomposition and erosion. The nutritive value of a soil patch is determined by the amounts and balance of these various substances. Plants need a soil rich in nutrients to satisfy their needs.

Because plants can only draw nourishment that is dissolved in water, plants need the kind of soil that can absorb and retain a supply of water. Without water, a plant cannot draw food from even the richest of soils, and it will die.

And soil must be loose enough to allow the unhampered circulation of oxygen. A plant's roots must have oxygen if they are to grow.

So soil is an earthen bank, holding reserves of food, water and oxygen vital to green life. Dry, compacted, alkaline or heavily acidic soil destroys all but the most adaptable of plant life.

In addition, the soil a house plant is potted in must have good drainage. Any water excess should be able to flow out of the pot. A compacted soil with poor drainage will retain too much water, possibly suffocating the roots or encouraging a rot to settle in.

So you have a plant that has outgrown the pot it arrived in. You've selected the pot, and now you need the soil. You inquire at the local garden center, and find yourself confronted with a baffling array of soil mixes.

Don't panic. Just read the labels.

Some soil mixes are formulated with one type of plant in mind, and such mixes will clearly state what plants they are intended for.

Many other mixes are made to be used for a variety of house plants, and the package should tell you that.

You can use most of these mixes as they come out of the bag, without additions. However, if a mix you select has a very high percentage of humus or peat moss, buy a bag of perlite as well. Humus is full of nutrients, but repeated waterings can turn a soil with a large amount of humus into a sticky mass. Congealed soil will strangle plant roots.

Perlite is a form of expanded volcanic rock. It will provide aeration and improve drainage in a pot by coarsening and forcing apart the particles of soil. Mix these small, pebbly rocks into the soil in the ratio of one part perlite to two parts soil mix.

Store mixes should see you through your plant apprenticeship. As you become more experienced, you can begin experimenting with soil mixes, buying the components and combining them in different percentages for different plants.

The elements a store mix—and a home mix—should have include:

Topsoil—which has nutritive elements, retains water but will become compacted when used without additions. A fifty-pound bag of topsoil will cost between $2 and $5.

Peat Moss—which has some nutritive value, but is really important because it provides aeration, absorbs water and increases the acidity of the soil. A four-foot bale of peat moss will cost from $3 to $12.

Humus—has many nutritive elements, and it holds moisture. If you use too much humus, you'll discover just how well it holds moisutre. A fifty-pound bag of humus generally costs about $5.

Perlite—is expanded volcanic rock. It provides aeration and drainage. Four cubic feet of perlite costs about $4.

Vermiculite—is a form of mica that has expanded under high temperatures. It provides drainage and retains moisture. When nutrients are dissolved in the moisture, vermiculite retains the liquid food and thus acts as a storehouse of nutrition for the plant. It costs approximately $4 for a large bag.

These are the basic ingredients of any homemade mix. Topsoil, perlite and humus are necessary components of any soil mix, while vermiculite and peat moss are helpful additions. Store mixes generally contain topsoil, humus and some perlite.

Every experienced gardener seems to have at least one soil recipe. Until you have mastered the basics of plant care and become thoroughly familiar with the differing needs of your plants, I suggest you stick to store-bought mixes. When you feel ready to experiment, consult the bibliography for a description of books dealing with advanced aspects of gardening. Or better yet, ask an experienced gardener.

I recommend experimentation. It's enjoyable, and you might develop a mix that will make all the difference to your plants. There is only one essential rule: never use a much larger percentage of any one of the elements in a mix. Doing so will lead to problems, for soil is a dynamic balance of elements. Upset the balance, and you run the risk of doing great harm to a plant.

SOIL ACIDITY AND ALKALINITY

You may have been puzzled by the references in plant books to soil acidity and alkalinity. What, you ponder, can *acids* have to do with house plants?

Quite simply, anything wet or water soluble contains some amount of the element hydrogen. Some materials can absorb and retain quantities of the element, while other materials hold much less. The materials commonly used in soil mixes hold varying amounts of hydrogen.

A predominance of hydrogen-rich materials in a soil mix will cause the soil to become alkaline. A soil compounded of materials having a low hydrogen content will become increasingly acidic.

House plants usually prefer a *slightly* acidic soil. However, very acidic or alkaline soil damages plants.

A soil test kit, sold in garden supply stores for as little as $5, can be used to test the hydrogen content of a soil. The kit will give you a pH reading, indicating the quantity of hydrogen in the soil. The reading may range from 0 to 14. A pH reading above 7 indicates sufficient hydrogen to turn a soil alkaline. A reading below 7 means there is a much smaller amount of hydrogen present, causing acidity.

A good reading for house plants would be somewhere between 6 and 7. However, some latitude is possible, and you should not become concerned unless a plant has the symptoms indicating too-acidic or too-alkaline soil.

Overly alkaline soil will cause leaves to become discolored, and it will stunt root development.

Soil that is too acidic is an infrequent occurence. When it does happen, leaves wilt and drop off.

These problems cannot be identified solely by their symptoms. Buy a soil test kit, and take pH readings for each plant several times a year.

If the test indicates a reading very much above or below 7, follow the directions printed on the kit's package to remedy the imbalance. You may have to turn a plant out and re-mix the soil, but restoring your plant's health is well worth the time.

Topsoil, humus and peat moss are acidic, while perlite and limestone are alkaline. An imbalance can be corrected by adding more acidic material to a strongly alkaline soil, or by adding alkaline material to an overly acidic soil—but don't just close your eyes and give it a try. *Follow the directions* printed on the test kit, or the information you draw from some other knowledgable source.

29

Chapter 5.
Plants and Food

House plants need regular applications of a fertilizer, or plant food, during their growing seasons. Plant foods contain an assortment of nutrients responsible for the healthy development of a plant.

Although the pasteurized soil in which you pot a plant will contain nutrients, its supply will soon be exhausted by the demands of a growing plant. In nature, nutrients are constantly replenished in the soil by the twin actions of decomposition and erosion. House plants have been removed from all such processes, and you must therefore personally assume the role of nature.

A plant receiving regular applications of fertilizer will look better, grow more rapidly and be much more resistant to infections or insects.

Nitrogen, phosphorus and potassium are the three elements of prime importance for a house plant. A "complete" fertilizer is any plant food having a balanced percentage of these three elements.

Their presence in a preparation will be indicated by a prominent listing of three percentages, as for instance 5-10-5 or 15-30-15.

Nitrogen is always represented by the first percentage. It is essential to the healthy growth of stems and leaves. Nitrogen is also an important element of chlorophyll, the substance that gives plant parts their distinctive green hue. An insufficient supply of nitrogen will slow the growth rate and cause plant parts to become stunted. Leaves may yellow, turn a wasted brown, or fall off. Too much nitrogen (which can happen when a plant has been overloaded with fertilizer) will unnaturally prolong a plant's growing period. Stems will be weakened, growth will droop and the plant may look as if it were suffering a breakdown. An exhausted plant becomes susceptible—even attractive—to diseases and pests.

WHO GETS WHAT?

Foliage plants—prefer plenty of nitrogen. Fish emulsion is an excellent source of nitrogen. Vary a nitrogen-rich food with a "well balanced" food.

Flowering plants—prefer plenty of phosphorus. Bone meal and superphosphate are excellent sources of phosphorus. Alternate applications with a food having nitrogen and potassium, as well as trace elements.

Azaleas, camellias, citrus, fruit plants and gardenias need plenty of acid in their diet. If they don't get enough, they can become chlorotic (See chapter 15). Some plant foods are especially formulated to supply extra acid. Don't give acid-loving plants a steady supply of such foods: give them a heavily acidic meal every three or four feedings.

30

Use a "complete" fertilizer and your plants will never have a shortage of nitrogen. A plant can only be overdosed with nitrogen when you feed it too often. If you have not been using a "complete" fertilizer, and a serious nitrogen deficiency has developed, you can correct it by treating a plant with doses of bone meal or fish emulsion, both of which are rich in nitrogen. Apply bone meal or fish emulsion to the soil, wait a week, and then begin regular applications of a "complete" fertilizer.

Phosphorus is always second on the list of percentages. It helps a plant produce strong, well-shaped roots and stems. It aids in the production of healthy flower buds, and it adds vividness to the shades of the flowers the buds produce. A phosphorus deficiency will cause a plant to stop growing. Quite strikingly, the leaves may turn a brighter and brighter shade of green, until they look as if they will explode and scatter green stuff around the room. Instead, they will become discolored, turning purple first and then assuming a badly mottled appearance.

Using a "complete" fertilizer will avoid such a deficiency and its cinematic symptoms. A severe shortage of phosphorus can be remedied by an application of bone meal.

Potassium is always represented by the third percentage figure listed on a plant food label. It gives a plant vigor, strengthens its stems and encourages the development of foliage. Leaves with severe tip burns, and plants shedding leaves from the base upwards indicate insufficient potassium.

Use a "complete" fertilizer and it won't happen.

Nitrogen, phosphorus and potassium are the most important (but not the only) nutrients a plant needs.

Plants also need calcium. They don't need it in the quantities they require any of the big three, but they do need some calcium on a regular basis. It adds strength and vigor to a plant's stems, roots and flowers. An inadequate supply of calcium will slow the growth rate, cause distorted leaves and produce blasted buds. Overly acidic soil decreases the amount of calcium available to a plant. Bone meal or limestone will lessen the acidity and also supply additional calcium.

A soil too low on the pH scale (See chapter 4) is too acidic, and interferes with the absorption of calcium. A soil test indication too high on the pH scale—meaning it is overly alkaline—interrupts the absorption of magnesium. Magnesium is a "trace element," one of a number of elements necessary for plant health, but required in very small quantities. Magnesium is a component of chlorophyll, and chlorophyll is a vital plant substance. Leaves browning in the center while they remain green along the margins indicate a magnesium shortage. Leaves might also whiten along their margins, or drop off.

31

If a plant exhibits any of the symptoms connected with calcium or magnesium deficiencies, or any of the symptoms mentioned in chapter 4 as indicating excessive alkalinity or acidity, test its soil with a soil test kit.

Magnesium deficiencies should not occur if you use an "organic" fertilizer. Organic fertilizers, such as fish emulsion, manure, bone meal, wood ashes or dolomitic limestone, contain largenpercentages of at least one of the "big three," and they are generally rich in trace elements. These elements, including iron, boron, copper, molybdenum, sulfur and zinc, are necessary for healthy plant growth, but in very small doses.

HOW TO READ THE LABELS

First of all, don't let the numbers printed on the label of each bag of plant food confuse you. The three numbers refer to the percentages of nitrogen, phosphorus and potassium (always in that order) contained in a mix. A 10-20-10 mix would have 10 percent nitrogen, 20 percent phosphorus and 10 percent potassium. In this case, 40 percent of the mix would be composed of the major elements, and the remaining 60 percent would be either trace elements or inert materials.

Plant foods come in a wide variety of percentages. You may find preparations listing 5-10-5 or 0-20-0 or 15-30-15. The 15-30-15 mix is one of the strongest foods you will find, as 60 percent of it consists of major elements. You might want such a strong food for some plants. For others, you might prefer a weaker blend.

Read the labels carefully. They will tell you exactly what a mix contains. If an element is not listed on the label, assume that the mix does not contain it. In addition, many manufacturers will declare what types of plants their mix is best suited for.

Chemical fertilizers generally carry large, balanced amounts of nitrogen, phosphorus and potassium. Some preparations may include trace elements, but many do not. Any mixture labeled as being "well balanced" will contain major *and* minor nutritive elements.

Until you become familiar with the varying needs of individual plants, I suggest the use of a "complete" fertilizer, with the addition of a mixture containing trace elements. You can accomplish this blend by varying your feedings: one time, use a "complete" plant food, and for the next application switch to a food featuring a good supply of trace elements. Turn it into a system, and it should not prove too confusing.

Plant foods are available in several forms. There are:

Liquids—Aside from specific organic liquids, liquids are chemical preparations concentrating on the "big three": nitrogen, phosphorus and potassium.

Slow-release tablets—Small white pills, they are made to be tucked into the soil mix. Supposedly, each watering will release a measured amount of fertilizer. They are not yet widely available.

Soluble powders—Powders are the most common, and probably the most convenient, of plant foods. They are available in a wide variety of formulas, and they can be measured exactly and dissolved in your watering can. You can feed when you water, a handy combination of procedures.

Tablets and sticks—Some gardeners swear by them, but others accuse them of attracting mold pockets while they are inserted in the soil surface. If you have a number of plants, you may lose track of when you put what tablet where.

I suggest the use of powders because you can easily keep track of your feeding schedule and you can combine feeding with watering, and because they are available in such a wide assortment of formulas.

But as with other aspects of plant care, your preferences are available time will prescribe your choice.

The most fundamental aspect of feeding a plant has been reserved for last. How *often* do you feed?

Less often than you might think.

First of all, feed your plants *only* during their seasons of growth. Stop feeding a plant when the seasons change and it is about to turn dormant. During the winter, plants in natural light need no food. If you continue to grow and flower plants throughout the year by using artificial light, of course you must continue to feed them.

Don't feed a plant exhibiting symptoms of distress. It will only compound the problem. Diagnose the trouble, and unless it is caused by a nutritional deficiency, do not feed the plant until the disease or pest has been eradicated.

Don't feed a plant you are about to transplant. And don't feed a plant for the first two weeks after you have transplanted it.

So how often *do* you feed?

The rough rule of thumb I suggest is to feed healthy flowering and foliage plants once every two or three weeks during their growing seasons. The frequency of feeding should be determined on the basis of your observations of the plant (does it seem content with what it is getting? does it need more, or is it showing signs of being gorged with what it has been getting?), the time of season (the more heat and light, the more rapidly food is consumed), and on the basis of the most convenient method for you.

Some indoor gardeners give a plant a *very* diluted dose of nutrients once a week. This, they suggest, insures that you never miss a plant, and prevents a "stop and start" pattern of growth caused by giving a plant a large meal every two to three weeks. Plant growth, they claim, spurts rapidly ahead after a feeding and then tapers off until the next meal. However, I have not observed such cyclic damage in plants regularly fed every other week. You may discover evidence to the contrary, and if you do I can only encourage you to follow the dictates of your own good sense and your plant's response.

Don't feed more than once a week under any circumstances. Your plants just do not need it, and will not know how to handle surplus nutrients. If you do feed every plant once a week, remember to dilute the solution substantially. All plant foods carry instructions for preparation and application, as well as exact measurements of amounts, printed on their packages. Follow them.

Don't feed plants on cool, overcast days, unless you are treating a deficiency.

FERTILIZER SALTS

If you apply fertilizer too frequently, or if a plant's soil is exhausted, you will get a build-up of fertilizer salts. A grimy crust coating the soil surface or collecting on the inner rim of a pot indicates salt build-up.

These salts burn roots, cause leaves to brown on their tips and margins, and interfere with a plant's intake and use of nutrients. Leaves may also become shrunken and malformed.

If you don't overfeed a plant, you'll rarely have this problem. If it does occur, cut back on the frequency of your applications of fertilizer. Give the affected plant several heavy waterings, one after the other, until the white crust has entirely disappeared. If watering does not dissolve all of the crust, transplant the plant to a clean pot and scrub the whitened pot in hot soapy water.

Salts are more likely to accumulate in pots without drainage holes, presenting a persuasive reason for using *only* pots having drainage holes. Plastic pots have salt build-ups more frequently, because their walls do not absorb the salts. The walls of clay pots do absorb quantities of fertilizer salts, often preventing any damage. You *could* use only clay pots, but in the long run it's much simpler and wiser to just be more cautious in feeding your plants.

Sometimes the problem occurs because of salts in the water. If you are certain that you feeding practices are not at fault, suspect your local water works. Thanks to water treatment plants, concentrations of salts rarely occur in water. However, if tap water is the source of your trouble, switch to distilled or spring water.

Chapter 6

Plants and Light

too much light   *inadequate light*

A plant needs light to convert the nutrients it draws from the soil into energy. That energy produces new plant growth.

Light may be the most misunderstood and neglected of all the plant care necessities. We give a plant too much light, assuming that since light is good, *more* light is even better. Or we give a plant too little light, believing that plants somehow can acquire the light they need from any point in a room. Such conflicting attitudes just are not so. Different plants need different amounts of light. And if they do not get the light they need, they may fail.

Know a plant's light needs before you buy it. Research the plant to learn if it needs bright or indirect light. And then take a good long look at your rooms. Can you supply the light this type of plant needs? Would you consider supplementing natural light by installing artificial lights? If you cannot give a plant the light it needs, don't buy it.

However, the situation is rarely that desperate. Most homes have a variety of light intensities available. You just have to know which plants to put in which windows.

Most plants need more light than we realize. Don't be misled by the healthy-looking plants you see in badly lit offices, banks or stores. Those plants are replaced repeatedly by contract with a plant supplier so that they always look as if they were doing wonderfully. Well, they are, and so would your collection if you replaced it every few months, or if you were a contract supplier.

Inadequate light over a long period will weaken plants and stunt their growth. Leaves will wilt and yellow, become discolored and fall off; flowers will fail to open, or open only partially to produce a withered bloom; young plants may assume bizarre shapes as they shed non-vital parts to conserve energy; mature plants often defoliate from the base upwards.

Giving a plant too much light is a rarer mistake, but just as deadly. An excessive amount of sunlight will scorch leaves, turning the parts of a leaf revealed to the light colorless, while the shadowed portions pale. Some plants wither and die in a few days under intense light. Other plants struggle on as we, judging them to need more water or food, gorge them with things they don't need. The light, food and water overstimulate plant processes, and may cause a plant to virtually shortcircuit and burn itself out. Young leaves are the first part of a plant to exhibit light damage. If you can locate no other cause for the peculiar things that are happening to new leaves, take a good look at the light a plant is getting.

The amount of light falling on a particular location is determined by day length and intensity. Day length is an estimate of the average number of hours a location receives sunlight each day. Intensity is an estimate of the amount and strength of light that falls upon a location.

You can determine light day lengths by using your watch and your powers of observation. Light intensity can be rapidly determined with the aid of a light meter.

For instance, the ideal location for a sun-loving plant would be a window with southern exposure, combining the longest day length with the greatest intensity.

Windows with an eastern or western exposure have shorter day lengths and lower intensities of light. Such windows receive morning or mid-afternoon sunlight, and get only very diffused light during the sun's peak hours of warmth. Windows facing north have the lowest day length and intensity ratings, as they receive diffused light through the entire day.

You cannot affect the day lengths of light falling on any window, but you can take advantage of them by moving plants to windows having day lengths of light closest to their needs. You can decrease intensity at a window by using curtains or a blind to filter sunlight. Or you can situate plants prefering a semi-sunny position behind a rank

36

of sun-loving plants. Intensity can often be increased by removing obstacles, such as curtains indoors or tall bushes and shrubs outdoors.

However, when an adjoining wall is quite close to one of your windows, you may get very little light, both of day length and intensity. If that is the case, relocate all of the plants except those preferring a semi-shady location. You will find that a wall covered

PLANTS AND THEIR LIGHT REQUIREMENTS

Most windowsills receive one of three intensities of light. These intensities include:

1. The amount of light falling on a window receiving plenty of bright diffused light, but no direct sunlight. Such a location would have a reading of from f 5.6 to f 8 on a light meter. Plants doing well in such a location include:
Adiantum, Aglaonema, Aspidistra, Dracaena, Dieffenbachia, Ficus, Kentia, Lygodium, Maranta, Nephthytis, Pandanus, Philodendron, Sansevieria and Zamia. While many foliage house plants do well in such a location, few flowering house plants will.

2. The amount of light found on a window receiving constant bright light, but no sunlight. A light reading taken at such a window would probably be near f 8. The plants listed below do well in such a location, and would find direct sunlight too harsh. Such plants include:
Acanthus, Araucaria, Ardisia, Asparagus, Begonia, Browallia, Caladium, Camellia, Chlorophytum, Coleus, Columnea, Cordyline, Crassula, Cyclamen, Dieffenbachia, Dracaena, Episcia, Fatsia, Fuchsia, Gardenia, Hedera, Monstera, Pleomele, Schefflera, Smilax, Tradescantia, Zebrina.

You'll notice that some plants are included in both lists. Most plants listed in either #1 or #2 will adapt to either light condition. However, it seems that most plants listed here do better exposed to the light level of #2.

3. The amount of light found on a window receiving several hours of direct sunlight. A light meter would register from f 11 to f 16 on a bright or very bright windowsill. Plants doing their best under such conditions include:
Abutilon, Acampe, Agave, Aloe, Amaryllis, Cactus, Crassula, Euphorbia, Eucalyptus, Fatshedera, Gynura, Hibiscus, Hoya, Kalanchoe, Ligustrum, Lantana, Pittosporum, Sydenium, Succulents, Trifolium and Vitis.

These lists are intended to demonstrate the general light level required by a wide range of plants. However, I would advise you to research specific plants to determine their exact light needs.
Generally, foliage house plants need bright to very bright *diffused* light, while flowering house plants need *some* direct sunlight (although not an entire day of it), and cacti and succulents need several hours of direct sunlight.

with a bright paint acts as a light reflector, bounding additional light into a window. Examine all of the conditions affecting the amount of sunlight your rooms receive, and arrange your plants accordingly.

Consult the lists appended to this chapter to locate plants that can adapt to the light available to your rooms. And take heart—there are plants for every kind of environment, from the dimmest of rooms to the very brightest.

Don't ignore a plant's light requirements. Know what they are, give them what they need, and you will never lose a plant to a severe case of sunburn, or see a plant wilt and die in the dimness of an obscure window.

Light is such a fascinating quality because you can use your ingenuity to alter it to your needs. And if all else fails, consider artificial lighting, fluorescent bulbs being the most frequently recommended light source. You can use it to supplement the sunlight you commonly get, or make it the single light source for your plants. Many plants do very well under artificial light, such lights can make all the difference between sterile, twilit rooms or a brilliant gathering of green life. Consult the bibliography for a listing of books explaining the techniques of engineering artificial light.

LIGHT LEVELS AND LIGHT METERS

You can arrive at a rough determination of the amount and intensity of light falling upon a window by using your powers of observation. A shrewd estimate should be sufficient, but if you are unsure, or if you feel that you need an exact measurement (you rarely will), use a light meter.

Photographers use light meters to gauge the amount of light falling upon a given location. Many cameras are now manufactured with built-in light meters, or they can be purchased separately. However, I believe rough approximations are sufficient for most occasions, and I certainly do not recommend the purchase of a light meter just to measure sunlight on a windowsill.

If you already own a light meter (or a camera with a light meter) or if you can borrow one from a friend, you can certainly try a meter reading. Otherwise, don't worry about it.

If you have obtained a meter, take your readings around noon, when the sun will be at its zenith.

Adjust the meter to an ASA film speed index of 200, and a shutter speed of 1/125th of a second.

Take a piece of plain white paper and place it at what you estimate to be the height of the upper foliage of a house plant.

Don't use a sheet of paper with a dull surface—use a sheet of typing paper.

Turn the sheet towards the source of light. You may need to recruit someone to hold the paper while you bring the meter close enough to it to eliminate the influence of any other light sources. Remember, you're reading the paper, not the windowsill or the room beyond. Take care not to cast a shadow on the sheet or to obscure the light source.

The meter will respond to the light by indicating the appropriate camera lens opening, such as f 5.6, f 8, or f 11. You then correlate those readings to a standard light intensity guide. Brooklyn Botanic Gardens publishes a handbook titled *Gardening Under Artificial Light* that includes a list of the amount of light necessary for various plants.

Chapter 7

Plants and Water

need of water

Plants need a regular supply of water. They should be watered regularly, but not too frequently—and not too infrequently, either.

Watering a plant too often will cause leaves to wilt or decay. Leaf tips may become brittle, while scabby bubbles develop on the undersides of leaves; rotting may begin in the roots, on the crown or along the stem; rots and the general disorder produced by overwatering provide entrance to pests and other infections.

Watering a plant infrequently will cause it to wilt badly; its soil may dry, pucker and pull back from the walls of the pot, until it is densely packed around the roots and plant stem; water will wash through the pot without ever reaching the roots; foliage will become increasingly discolored; stems and leaves will wither and turn pale; some plants will rapidly defoliate.

Now there is no one single easy all-inclusive rule to be strictly followed in watering. But there are guidelines, and you can adapt them to the needs of individual plants.

These guidelines can be considered as parts of two separate questions:

How often should you water?

And how much water should you give a plant?

How often you water depends on the specifics of the situation. It depends on the type of plant, the time of year, the temperature, light and humidity levels, the density of the soil, and the type of pot a plant has.

40

Some plants have very definite water requirements. Cacti and some succulents (including begonias and some euphorbias) prefer to have waterings spaced far enough apart to allow the soil to thoroughly dry out each time.

Other plants, such as citrus, camellia, dieffenbachia, dracaenas, ferns, and gardenias require soil that is constantly moist during their periods of growth. They should be watered often enough to keep the soil constantly moist—though not waterlogged.

Fortunately, most house plants are much more adaptable. The guideline for watering them is to give them water when the topsoil has lost its moistness, but before the soil becomes very dry.

Plants need more water during their growing seasons than during their periods of dormancy. Plants also need to be watered more often during periods of warm, sunny weather. One homely rule I've heard says that the larger the leaf surface, and the faster the growth rate, the more frequent the waterings should be.

A general rule is that during the spring and summer, most plants should be watered once a week. Plants needing constantly moist soil should be watered every several days. But, once again, there is no simple answer. You must adjust your waterings to the needs of particular plants as you come to understand those needs.

During the fall and winter plants need much less water. Dormant plants should be watered no more than two to three times a month. They simply don't need much water. Give them more than they can handle, and you can damage the roots or encourage the spread of a rot. But if you are gardening under lights, or if for any reason your plants remain active, water them as you would during the summer, adjusting the frequency according to the variables mentioned above.

On very humid days plants do not need any water, as they can draw sufficient moisture from the air. Watering would only make a plant susceptible to fungus infections.

Any time of year, a plant in direct sunlight needs to be watered more often than a plant in a dimmer location.

Heavy soils, being those soils with a large percentage of peat moss or humus, retain moisture longer and a plant potted in a heavy soil needs to be watered less often than a plant potted in a light, airy soil.

A plant in a large pot needs to be watered less often than the same plant in a smaller pot. A potbound plant will suffer from a chronic thirst, as it will have less soil and be unable to retain water for any length of time. Clay pots speed evaporation, as the water can flow through the drainage holes and can evaporate from both the soil surface and the walls of the pot. Water in plastic pots can only pass through the drainage holes or evaporate from the soil surface.

Because clay is porous, water a plant in a clay pot more frequently than the same plant in a plastic pot.

If you can, I suggest that you water your plants in the morning, as they will require reserves of moisture during the hours of growth when they are exposed to sunlight.

There is no single answer to how often you should water. But keep these variables in mind, match them with your observations of the environment your plants exist in, consult the chart following this chapter, and you should be able to work out an appropriate schedule.

But make it a *flexible* schedule, based on all you have observed of the variables described above.

I can give a much simpler answer to the question: how much water should you give your plants?

Give them plenty. Give each and every plant a long and thorough watering. If the pot sits on a saucer, give the plant water until you see it running into the saucer. Or, if the pot has no saucer, water the plant until the topsoil appears saturated. Some gardeners make it a rule to fill up the space between a plant's soil surface and the rim of its pot. Then they move on to the next plant and return when the water has percolated through. If a plant still looks thirsty, they give it another draught. A half hour to an hour after you water, return and empty the excess out of each saucer.

If a plant shows symptoms of overwatering, reduce the frequency of your waterings immediately. Prune rotted roots and remove any damaged leaves. Put the plant in a light, well-ventilated spot to recover, and don't water again until the soil looks thoroughly dry.

Give a plant a good long drink each time you water and it will never suffer damage from underwatering. Unless, of course, you keep forgetting to water it at all.

How should you water?

You can water from above, from below or use the wick method.

Top watering is the fastest method. Use a long spouted watering can to push through the foliage and evenly soak the soil surface. Don't just dump the spout down and let it flow—apply the water with a gentle, even motion. And don't water the foliage—water only the soil, and the moisture will eventually get back to the leaves. If you want to, you can mist the leaves several times a week, but when you come around with a watering can, be sure to use it to water the soil.

To water from the bottom, immerse a pot to just *below* its soil line in a container of water. The water should be at room temperature. Capillary action will draw the water up into the soil. When the soil surface becomes moist and glistens with beads of water, the plant has had enough.

42

Always water plants that have sustained damage from underwatering by this method. The soil of parched plants may have drawn away from the sides of the pot, and water applied from above would simply run through without soaking the soil or roots.

Some gardeners prefer to water all their plants by this method because they can tell exactly when their plants have had enough. However, unless you have a small collection of plants or a great deal of free time, you probably won't find this method suitable. Of course, you can always reserve it for those special plants that require exacting attention. If you do water more than one plant from below, remember to change the water. Otherwise, you might innocently be passing some green social disease along.

Allow plants to drain thoroughly before returning them to their accustomed spots. And do water your seedlings from below. They seem to prefer it, and you'll be certain of giving them the water they need.

Wick watering should be used *only* on plants that require a constant supply of moisture at their roots. Commercial models can be quite expensive, although you can construct a home model that will do the job. (See insert.)

Watering your plants should present no problems as long as you follow the basics and use your powers of observation to adjust the frequency of waterings to the varying needs of your plants.

And remember, always give them a good long drink.

HOW TO WICK WATER

Wick watering should be used *only* on those plants requiring a constant supply of moisture, such as camellia, citrus, dieffenbachia, dracaenas, ferns and gardenias. And while it is an especially efficient method of watering such plants, it is not mandatory. Just water such plants every few days during their growing periods, so that the soil never dries out. But *don't* let the soil become waterlogged!

You can purchase a wick waterer, or you can make your own.

Wick watering is a simple, but ingenious idea. A length of material, such as nylon stockings, capable of absorbing and transmitting moisture is inserted into a pot through a drainage hole and drawn up halfway into the pot. An equal amount of wick should extend below the pot.

Follow the normal potting procedure, filling the pot with drainage material, soil and a plant. Then fill a deep, wide saucer with clean pebbles and push the free end of wick all the way down through the

wick watering

pebbles to the base of the saucer. Stand the pot on top of the pebbles, then fill the saucer with water. The wick should supply the lower half of the pot and the plant's roots with a steady amount of water.

Water the plant once from above, and then water again from above only if the wick seems not to be working.

Remember, the pot should be standing on top of the pebbles, and not in the water.

I've seen homemade wick units that work very well, but they do take a bit of experimentation to get just the right supply of water. You might want to try this method on a plant requiring constant moisture, or you can just be more diligent in watering from above. It's up to you.

WATER REQUIREMENTS

While the frequency of watering a plant is largely determined by different variables, most house plants can be classified in three categories:

1. Plants requiring constant moisture. Never let the soil dry out, but do not water so frequently as to cause the soil to become waterlogged. Such plants include: Camellia, Citrus, Dieffenbachia, Dracaena, Ferns and Gardenias.

2. Plants that should be watered after the soil surface has turned dry, but before the rest of the soil has dried out. Plants in this category include: Aglaonema, Aspidistra, Ardisia, Asparagus, Cissus, Cordyline, Dieffenbachia, Fittonia, Gynura, Maranta, Podocarpus and Tradescantia.

3. Plants that should be watered as soon as an additional layer under the surface has dried out. You can determine this by gently prodding the soil with your finger. Such plants include: Agave, Aucuba, Crassula, Croton, Euphorbia, Ficus, Hoya, Pittosporum, Pleomele, Philodendron and Schefflera.

Remember that these lists are only approximations—research your plants for specific watering needs1 and vary the frequency of watering to accord with other conditions such as soil type and room temperature.

44

Chapter 8
Plants and Humidity

Plants need humidity, and a goodly measure of it, in order to prosper. Although our environment may seem quite comfortable to us, it may feel only slightly more humid than the Gobi desert to a sensitive plant.

Most rooms simply do not have sufficient levels of humidity. If you intend to grow anything other than the hardiest of plants, you must take care to add moisture to the air circulating around plants. And no, extra waterings will not do the job.

insufficient humidity

When a plant has not been receiving sufficient humidity, its leaves may brown at the tip, yellow along the margins or drop off in large numbers. Buds shrivel and fall away. If you do not increase the humidity available to the plant, it may fail. Also, in such a weakened state a plant will often be incapable of resisting disease of infestation.

Plants transpire. People perspire.

The process may differ, but the principle is the same.

When we perspire, water evaporates off the surface of our skin in an effort to stabilize our body temperature.

Plants transpire in an attempt to add more moisture to their environment. On a warm summer day, or a dry winter's day, there will be little moisture available in most rooms. Your plants must draw moisture up from their roots and transpire it, but their supply of water is limited, and once it is exhausted the dry air will turn leaves brown or defoliate the plants.

If we spend any length of time in rooms having a low humidity level, our eye, nose or throat membranes may become irritated.

If a plant spends any length of time in a room having little moisture in the air, it may become damaged or die.

So plants need more humidity than most rooms contain. What is humidity? And how can we increase the moisture content of the air in our rooms?

Humidity is water suspended in the air as a vapor. The term "relative humidity" refers to the percentage of moisture in the air sampled at the specific location, as measured against the total amount of moisture this air can hold without the vapor being precipitated into rain or fog. A reading of 50% humidity would indicate that the air sampled contained half of the moisture it could carry without that moisture condensing and becoming visible.

Warm air can sustain greater amounts of humidity without precipitating. A temperature of 72°, matched with 40% humidity (a good match for house plants) would carry more humidity than a temperature of 52° and 40% humidity.

House plants do their best in an atmosphere having between 40% and 60% humidity. During the summer months, the air should carry sufficient moisture to satisfy your plants. But during the winter, many house plants are subjected to atmospheres from which almost all of the humidity has been removed. Most modern heating systems wring the humidity out of air, leaving it warm and bone dry. It is common for the humidity levels in heated rooms to drop as low as 10% to 12%.

A hygrometer will help you determine the extent of your problem. Hygrometers can measure the relative humidity of a room; they are small, simple to use and inexpensive (as little as $5). If you are quite serious about raising and displaying plants, it will be invaluable. So get a hygrometer, and use it.

You take readings, and are dismayed to learn how little moisture there is in the air. What do you do to remedy the situation?

If you own your own home, and if you can afford an outlay of several hundred dollars, you can have a humidifier installed as part of the heating system. That should go a long way towards resolving the trouble. But if you rent an apartment, or you just can't afford to spend that much money, there are many inexpensive alternatives.

Buy a room humidifier. Such units cost between $25 and $100, and they may supply all the moisture your plants need.

Buy a vaporizer. They don't produce *that* much humidity, but anything will help. Put a vaporizer close enough to your plants to help them, yet not so close that they might be scalded by occasional drops of warm water. I personally consider a vaporizer no more than an emergency aid, and recommend that you don't attempt to use one for any length of time. Just use it to postpone further damage while you work out a better environment.

Bring your plants together. Their mutual deep breathing will add moisture to their collective environment and will benefit them all. Your plants don't need another drink—they need moisture in the air around them.

If you have the room, consider putting several pots in a large planter. Line the bottom of the planter with a thick layer of humus or peat moss, and place the individual pots directly into it. By keeping the material constantly moist (though *not* saturated) you can generate a good steady amount of moisture in the atmosphere around the plants. But don't assume that just putting plants in such a container is the answer. Get out your trusty hygrometer, and check to be sure. If it is not enough, use other methods to supplement the process.

The use of large trays is often suggested as a remedy for insufficient humidity. The trays should be made of some rustproof material, and have walls at least ½" in height. Line the bottom of the trays with one or two layers of small, smooth pebbles or perlite, and stand the pots on the gravel. Pour water in until it reaches three-quarters of the height of the gravel. The bases of the pots must not sit in the water—they must be just above it. Otherwise, roots may be suffocated or begin to rot. As the water evaporates, it provides a steady supply of humidity to the plants.

Do not use shards of brick or other materials you might have scavenged in place of the perlite or pebbles. They may contain large amounts of alkaline substances that will be leached into the water. Then if you pour in too much water, the alkalines may reach—and badly burn—a plant's roots.

Maintain a constant supply of water in the trays, and make certain that the pots on either end of each tray are not so close to the edges that foliage hangs over or away from the tray. If that happens, some of the foliage will entirely miss the benefits of the continual evaporation, and that foliage will yellow or wilt. Don't crowd a tray. Put on it only as many pots as can be accommodated without crowding.

Ferns and some tropical plants thrive in the humid atmosphere of a bathroom. They make a lively addition to the room, but make sure that you can give them the light they need, as well as the humidity. One devoted indoor gardener I know has packed his bathroom with plants. Some hang suspended from the ceiling in baskets, while others are displayed on racks lining the walls. Large plants are lined in a row along one wall, and the bathtub is almost entirely overgrown with green life. Ferns and vines twist so densely downwards that he cannot shower. But when he slips into the tub for a bath, he assures me, it is rather like floating in a tropical stream surrounded by luxuriant growth. Of course, he uses large banks of artificial lights to nurture this growth, and his electric bills must be substantial. It is the densest, most exotic display of house plants I have ever seen.

Spray or mist plant leaves regularly. Hand-operated sprayers are available in many colors and sizes, ranging in price from $2 up to $15. Spray each plant several times a week, and try to spray in the morning. Don't burden foliage with great dollops of water—a mist is suitable. Be certain to spray the entire plant, and not just one side. On very warm summer days, you can spray once again in the afternoon, but never spray a plant after the sun has set. And don't spray a plant sitting in direct sunlight, as the water may bead on the leaves. These beads will focus and concentrate the sun's rays, and a bad leaf burn may result. Fill your sprayer with water at room temperature. You can protect walls and furniture by placing a piece of cardboard behind a plant as you spray it.

Spraying plant leaves will not substantially increase the level of humidity, but it will help.

48

Wiping foliage down with a damp cloth or sponge will serve the same purpose, but it is a tedious process, and even a soft cloth can scratch a leaf.

You know the basics—now go to work with your imagination to invent other methods of increasing humidity around plants.

If the problem is chronic, and nothing seems to work, fashion yourself a small home greenhouse. Use a sheet of plastic to seal off an entire windowsill. Water the parched plants and put them out the windowsill. Tack the plastic closed. Pin back a corner of the sheet once or twice every day for a half hour to air out the windowsill. In the meantime go to work on adding moisture to the room, and when you have succeeded, or when a plant has recovered, bring the plant, or plants, back into the room.

An oversupply of humidity can be a problem during warm, damp weather. However, this is a rare problem, usually confined to coastal areas. While humidity is not directly damaging, it can further the development of molds, mildews and other diseases. Damaged plants will thus exhibit white or gray growths, rotted, mushy tissue or discolored leaves. Cacti, roses and any of the plants commonly used in terrariums are most likely to suffer an infection caused by a prolonged period of high humidity.

The problem is rare, but if you believe the potential does exist, increase the ventilation in the room. Open the door, open all the windows or use a fan. Just be certain that none of the plants are standing in a draft. Until the weather moderates, reduce the frequency of your waterings. Better yet, use an air conditioner (for both you and the plants).

You can improve the humidity in a room by using the techniques given here, or using your imagination to create other techniques. Your plants will demonstrate their appreciation by producing glossy, fresh, exuberant green growth.

Chapter 9.

Plants and Temperatures

Yes, most house plants are descended from tropical plants. Their wild relatives grow in conditions of great warmth and high humidity.

Yes, most house plants are grown in greenhouses maintaining constantly high temperatures to spur plant growth.

But no, you should *not* attempt to duplicate such temperatures in your home. You may be able to generate the heat, but there is no way you can match the light and humidity levels maintained constantly in greenhouses, short of building one yourself.

And heat without humidity is murder on house plants. They will wilt, stop growing and may even defoliate under the pressure of high temperatures. In addition, plants in such a weakened state are vulnerable to disease or insect infestations.

Reputable greenhouse men "harden off" their stock by giving them gradually increasing exposures to a normal environment. By the time they are delivered to plant shops, most plants should be hardy enough to rapidly adjust to the temperatures prevailing in your home. But they will do their best in rooms having temperatures no higher than 75° throughout the year, and no lower than 55° during the spring and summer. During the winter, some plants can adjust, and may even prefer lower temperatures. Consult the accompanying chart for the temperature requirements of some popular plants.

too hot

If the temperature of a room is too high for a plant, its leaves will wilt, yellow and fall off. Such damage also makes a plant susceptible to insects or infections. And if you water to alleviate the trouble without correcting the temperature, a plant's roots may begin to rot away.

50

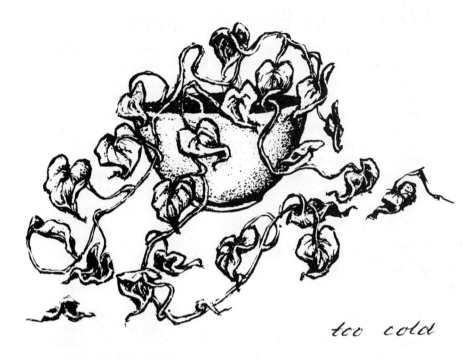

too cold

Plants suffering from an exposure to temperatures colder than they can adapt to will wilt. Their leaves will curl, become discolored or entirely brown, and fall off.

Most plants prefer a drop of from 10° to 15° in temperature during the night. Plants grown in office buildings often suffer because they are given just the opposite during their growing months. The air conditioners pump out cold air during the day, but they are turned off in the evening and the plants must spend a warm night. Such switches addle them and adversely affect their growth.

Try to avoid sudden increases or decreases in room temperatures. Plants *are* hardy, but they need time to adjust to changes. So if you come into a room that has been unheated through a winter's day, don't push the thermostat all the way up, and don't build a roaring fire in that attractive fireplace. Push the thermostat up gradually, and remove any plants from the immediate vicinity of a fireplace before you build a fire.

During the fall, inspect your windowsills for any cracks admitting cool drafts and seal any you discover. And move back any plants brushing window panes with their foliage. On very cold nights that foliage can be fatally chilled. You might even place a sheet of cardboard between a windowpane and the plants on a windowsill during very cold nights.

51

If you display plants in trays placed on top of radiators, line the trays with an extra layer of gravel, allowing additional water. And never let the water level in the trays fall. Never, *never*, put a pot directly onto a radiator or other heated surface. Such warmth could kill a plant overnight.

Remember, house plants do not need the heat their wild relatives thrive in. Protect them from extremes of heat and cold. Give them moderate temperatures.

Don't underestimate the hardiness of your plants. They fall ill, remember, when *we* do the wrong thing to them. Give them what they need, and *only* what they need, and they should do quite well.

HOUSE PLANT TEMPERATURE REQUIREMENTS

Most house plants will grow healthfully in a room having a temperature that does not exceed 75° F. during the day, nor fall below 55° at night.

There are, however, some exceptions. Aglaonema and Dieffenbachia can be damaged by temperatures falling lower than 60°; Begonias, Coleus, Maranta, Pandanus and Roheo can be traumatized by temperatures lower than 55°; but many other house plants can easily accept an occasional dip into the low 50's.

Some hardy plants *prefer* temperatures that climb no higher than 65° F. during the day. Such plants include Acacia, Aucuba, Azalea, Camellia, Cyclamen, Fatshedera, Fatsia, Fuchsia, Hedera, Ligustrum, Lantana, Primula and Streptocarpus.

Research the temperature preferences of your plants. If you can, separate those needing lower temperatures and grow them in a cooler, though sunny, spot.

The majority of plants will be perfectly comfortable in your rooms, so long as the temperature does not climb above 75° or consistently fall below 55°.

Chapter 10

Plants and Ventilation

Fresh air is a tonic to house plants. It strengthens plant stems and increases plant vigor. It also clears rooms of household odors potentially harmful to plants.

During moderate weather, regularly air any rooms containing house plants. Open either a door or windows, but make certain that the plants are not exposed to drafts (fast-moving currents of cool air). Sudden drafts of cool air can traumatize a plant, causing leaves to curl, brown or fall off in large numbers.

Gas fumes and the odor of fresh paint are also injurious to plants. When you paint a room, don't just cover your plants—move them out and keep them out until the aroma of paint has dissipated.

If you keep plants in your kitchen, and if you use manufactured gas for your stove, open a window or use a fan to ventilate the room while you are cooking. All of the gas is not burned off when in use; some of it escapes into the air, and a sufficient amount will cause leaves to brown, wilt or wither and will even kill plants. Jerusalem cherry and tomato plants are especially susceptible to gas damage. If any plant seems to be doing badly in your kitchen, relocate the plant to some other room. I have been told that plants having thick, leathery leaves are unaffected by gas fumes, and you might want to test this observation.

The smoke produced by a cosy fire can turn the edges and tips of leaves a wasted brown. Leaves may also become discolored and drop off. In severe cases, a plant suffering smoke damage may die. However, since most fireplaces are well ventilated, little smoke will escape into the room and plants will not be harmed. If a plant does exhibit smoke damage, move it into another room until the fireplace is no longer in use.

You may have heard that tobacco smoke harms plants. It does—but only when it is present in far greater quantities than one would find in most homes. When you give a party, move any plants you suspect of having an allergy to smoke to some more secluded area. They will be protected not only from fumes and ashes, but from the rough examinations of curious guests.

You may also have heard that a bowl of ripening apples placed in a room having a number of plants will have a palpably bad effect on the plants. Incredibly, it is true! The apples give off enough ethylene gas to blanch or yellow plant leaves. So keep your ripening apples in plant-less rooms.

Your plants need fresh air. Give it to them—in moderation. Protect them from drafts, and take precautions whenever you think harmful fumes might have been generated in your home.

Chapter 11
Pollution

Air pollution can injure and even kill house plants. Delicate, thin-leaved plants (such as ferns) seem especially susceptible to pollution damage.

Urban and industrial areas often have concentrations of chemical wastes in the surrounding atmosphere. These harsh, invisible chemicals can discolor clothing, corrode the strongest materials, and cause eye and respiratory problems. Pollutants can singe the tips and edges of plant leaves, turning them brown and brittle; or the leaves may turn yellow and drop in large numbers. Soot or greasy dust may settle in quantities on leaves. Such grit can cause discoloration, wilting and even defoliation. New growth may be stunted, or emerge malformed. A plant reacting to severe pollution may cease growing, and some plants may even die. For example, ferns damaged by air pollution can fail within two days of their first exposure.

The effects of pollution are often intensified by high temperatures and excessive humidity. If you live in a city, or if you live within fifty miles of a large industrial area, take special precautions to protect your plants on hot, humid days. Open a door, use a fan or open several windows to increase the circulation within a hot, stuffy room. Such ventilation helps to dissipate and disperse smog or invisible particles of pollution. It also serves to lower the humidity level. Water your plants less often during periods of hot, sticky weather. When you do water, be sure beads of moisture are not allowed to stand on leaves—they focus and collect dust and pollution particles, as well as encouraging rots. Keep leaves clean by regularly misting them.

If you can afford an air conditioner, it will filter some pollution and much of the dust out of the air in one or two rooms. It will also reduce the humidity and lower the temperature. If you can't afford one, just be more vigilant in caring for your plants when temperatures and pollution levels climb.

If your area suffers from consistently high pollution levels, consider buying only hardy, thick-leaved plants. Foliage house plants seem to be less affected by pollution than flowering house plants.

Never assume a plant is suffering from pollution until you have thoroughly investigated all other possibilities. But if you can find no evidence of insects or infection, you can conclude that your plant is a victim of future shock.

Chapter 12

Children and Animals

ANIMALS

House plants plus house pets sometimes equal trouble. Plants that have smashed to the floor without apparent cause, foliage that disappears overnight, and excavated root systems are symptoms of attention from curious or frustrated house pets.

Although birds and dogs may damage plants, the majority of cases I've heard about concern cats:

—Cats that decide to use a large plant's soil surface as the site of their afternoon naps. The soil may become compacted, and insufficient water will percolate through the roots.

—Cats that mistake plant soil for their litter boxes. The wastes may burn tender root systems.

—Cats that sample plant leaves for a change of diet.

—Cats that shove aside plants taking up a sunny spot on a windowsill.

If you have a cat, give pussy a windowsill spot all her own. If your cat develops a taste for a particular kind of plant, keep it out of kitty's way. Put the plant on a rack that cat can't reach. If the problem is serious, give your cat a plant of her own to toy with, or cease growing the type of plant that attracts the most feline attention. I've been told that a bit of catnip dropped on the soil of frequently molested plants will repel cats for several weeks at a time, but I hesitate to recommend the procedure. I just don't like to add anything to a plant's soil that it doesn't absolutely need. Use your wits to handle your cat by transfering your plants to racks above a cat's reach, or going in heavily for hanging plants.

Adult dogs seem unmoved by plants, but a friendly bushy tail might inadvertently topple a plant. Keep your plants as far away from sill edges as possible—your elbow can knock off a plant as easily as an enthusiastic pet. Teething puppies sometimes might sample a plastic pot, or even foliage, so keep plants well out of puppy paths.

Pet birds allowed out of their cages occasionally slice away parts of house plants to which they take a fancy. So if you sometimes parole your pet birds, remove any house plants from the room they'll be exploring.

There is another very good reason for taking precautions with your house plants. Some plants, such as dieffenbachia, oleander and poinsettias, have poisonous leaves. A session with these plants can be fatal to a curious pet. Always keep such plants, as well as any other plants you suspect of being dangerous, far out of orbit of your pets.

CHILDREN

Children are a very good reason for keeping potentially harmful plants well out of reach. They might sample a leaf or scoop up a small handful of soil. Neither substance will agree with them.

They might also topple carelessly placed plants over onto themselves. If you have small children, foresight should prevent such problems.

However, if you enjoy plants, you would be well advised to share that pleasure with children. I think you will find that most children are fascinated by the process of growth, and by the appearence of brilliant or bizarre plants. The growth of a house plant from seedling to maturity offers a clear, detailed lesson in the workings of natural life.

In addition, the care of a special plant can be a source of pride in accomplishment for a child. Help your child (or children) to take a cutting and root it in sterile soil. As the seedling matures, teach them how to gently transplant it into a larger pot. Teach them the basics of good plant care. Their questions may tax your knowledge and send you back to the plant books. Certainly such a project should prove satisfying for both of you. And it might start a youthful gardener on a lifelong activity, as well as encourage an appreciation of nature and the delicate relationships of life forms.

Right now, nature can use all of the appreciation it can get.

Now—what plants are suitable for children?

They should be hardy types.

Remember that children might be more interested in a bizarre or striking plant, such as a Venus flytrap or a voodoo (sacred lily of India) plant.

They might enjoy coleus, or any number of plants having brilliant colors or unusual foliage.

Children and plants *can* co-exist. Take precautions when they're little; when they are old enough to want to, then introduce them to plant life.

Chapter 13
"Away With All Pests"

There are some 100,000 species of insects inhabiting North America. Of that number, perhaps several thousand species prove harmful to crops, green life, or through toxins, to man. Yet that relatively small number account for billions of dollars of damage every year.

No more than two dozen species of insects commonly attack house plants. But those two dozen can quickly strip the leaves from a plant, drain its vital juices or gnaw its roots until it fails. If unchecked, an infestation can pass from plant to plant, damaging or destroying an entire collection.

These house plant pests may enter your house as eggs hidden in unpasteurized soil; some may enter clutching your clothes, or curled in the clots of soil still on your garden tools; others may, quite simply, fly or clamber through an open window; very often, they find their way in through the myriad cracks and crevices that are part of any house or apartment building.

Once inside, hidden eggs may respond to warmth by hatching, delivering a huge hungry generation onto your juicy plants. Mature insects will seek out the plant parts they prefer, either burrowing into the soil to chew on roots, settling themselves on leaf undersides, along stems or in flowers, or scouting out a daylight refuge under pots or saucers, in piles of organic refuse, in furniture, or in dark corners.

Destruction is the symptom of an insect attack. Leaves turn yellow or brown, jagged holes appear in foliage, plants wilt and cease growing. Some species smear a honeydew-like substance on plants, attracting ants and providing a medium for the growth of a sooty mold. Tiny bumps or blisters may appear on plant parts. Small, coarse cobwebs may be spun across leaf axils.

Insects are elusive creatures. Some pests are too small to be observed, while others remain hidden in plant soil. Many emerge only at night, to ravage a plant and leave you puzzled after dawn.

Proper sanitation and plant care can prevent many insect attacks. But if a plant does begin to fail, even after you've made certain all other factors are correct, examine it to determine specific symptoms of damage, and match those symptoms against the descriptions of damage given in this chapter.

If, indeed, bugs bug you, and if the insects are large enough to be handled, pick them off of an infested plant. A stream of lukewarm water, or a scrubbing session with soapy water, is sufficient to dislodge some species. Relatively mild pesticides will end most infestations and prevent renewed attacks, only for the most persistent of insect troubles should you consider using lethal pesticides. Never over-react by laying down a chemical barrage.

We begin this chapter with a list of popular house plants and the insects they commonly attract. Although many insects have very specific tastes, this list is not meant to be the final, conclusive word. If the opportunity occurs, some insects will gladly enlarge their diet by sampling a new species of plant. However, given the choice, most pests will return again and again to specific types of plants. If your plant is not included in the list, observe the symptoms and appearance of the insect troubling your plant, and examine the insect profiles given in this chapter.

Whatever pest your plant has, the insect profiles offer a brief description, and detailed instructions for treating an attack.

The chapter concludes with an explanation of the various types of pesticides, what they do, how well they do, the relative danger involved, and how to apply them.

If you have plants you *will*, at some point, have insects. But an attack need not be fatal. Most house plants pests can be dealt with quickly, thoroughly, and without danger to you or further damage to the weakened plant.

ACUBA— *Mites*
AFRICAN VIOLETS— *Ants, Aphids, Leaf Miners, Mealybugs, Mites, Nematodes*
AGLAONEMA— *Ants, Mealybugs*
ANNUALS— *Leaf Rollers, Mites, White Fly*
ANTHURIUM— *Mites*
ARALIA— *Ants, Aphids, Mites, Scale, Thrips*
ARAUCARIA— *Mites*
ARDESIA— *Ants, Mites, Scale*
ASPARAGUS— *Ants, Aphids, Ferns*
ASPIDISTRA— *Ants, Mites, Scale*
AVOCADO— *Ants, Aphids, Mealybugs, Scale, Thrips*
AZALEA— *Ants, Leaf Miners, Scale, Thrips, White Fly*

BEGONIA— *Ants, Aphids, Leaf Rollers, Thrips*
BROMELIADS— *Ants, Scale*
BROWALLIA— *Leaf Miners, White Fly*

CACTI— *Ants, Mealybugs, Scale, Slugs, Snails, Sowbug*

CAMELLIA— *Ants, Scale, Millipedes (Symphylan)*
CHRYSANTHEMUM— *Ants, Aphids, Scale, White Fly*
CISSUS— *Ants, Mealybugs, Mites*
CITRUS— *Ants, Aphids, Mealybugs, Mites, Nematodes, Scale, Thrips, White Fly*
COFFEE PLANT— *White Fly*
COLEUS— *Ants, Mealybugs, White Fly*
COLUMNEA— *Ants, Leaf Miners, Mealybugs, Mites, Nematodes*
CORDYLINE— *Mites*
CRASSULA— *Ants, Mealybugs, Nematodes*
CROTON— *Mites*
CYCLAMEN— *Ants, Aphids, Mites, Thrips*

DIEFFENBACHIA— *Ants, Aphids, Mealybugs, Mites*
DIZYGOTHECA— *Ants, Mealybugs*
DRACAENAS— *Ants, Mealybugs, Mites*

EPISCIA— *Ants, Leaf Miners,*

Mealybugs, Mites, Nematodes
EUONYMUS— Ants, Scale

FATSHEDERA— Ants, Aphids
FATSIA— Ants, Aphids, Mites
FERNS— Ants, Aphids,
Mealybugs, Scale, Thrips, White
Fly
FICUS— Ants, Aphids,
Mealybugs, Mites, Scale, Thrips
FITTONIA— Ants, Leaf Miners,
Mealybugs, Mites, Nematodes
FUCHSIA— Ants, Aphids, Mites,
Thrips, White Fly

GARDENIA— Ants, Aphids,
Mealybugs, Mites, Nematodes,
Scale
GERANIUM— Ants, Aphids, Leaf
Rollers, Mites, Nematodes, White
Fly
GESNERIADS— Ants, Aphids,
Leaf Miners, Mealybugs, Mites,
Nematodes
GLOXINIA— Thrips
GYNURA— Ants, Aphids

HERBS— Ants, Mealybugs, Mites,
White Fly
HIBISCUS— Ants, Aphids,
Mealybugs, Mites, Scale
HOYA— Ants, Mealybugs,
Nematodes

IVIES— Ants, Aphids, Mealybugs,
Mites, Scale

JERUSALEM CHERRY— Ants,
Scale, Thrips, White Fly
JESSAMINE— Ants, Scale

LANTANA— Ants, Mealybugs,
White Fly
LIGUSTRUM— Ants, Scale

MARANTA— Mites
MYRTLE— Ants, Scale, Thrips

OLEANDER— Ants, Leaf Rollers,
Mealybugs, Scale

PALMS— Ants, Aphids,
Mealybugs, Mites, Nematodes,
Scale
PHILODENDRON— Mites,
Symphylan
PICK-A-BACK— White Fly
PITTOSPORUM— Ants,
Mealybugs, Scale
PODOCARPUS— Ants,
Mealybugs, Mites, Nematodes,
Scale
POINSETTIA— Ants, Aphids,
Mites
POMEGRANATE— Ants, Scale,
White Fly

ROSES— Leaf Rollers, Mites,
Thrips

SCHEFFLERA— Ants, Mealybugs,
Mites, Scale
SEA GRAPE— Ants, Aphids
SEEDLINGS— Ants, Crickets,
Cutworms, Sowbugs, Springtails
SMILAX— Ants, Mites, Scale,
White Fly
SPIDER PLANT— Mites
SUCCULENTS— Ants,
Mealybugs, Slugs, Snail, Sowbugs
SYNGONIUM— Mites

ZAMIA— Ants, Scale

IN GENERAL:
Caterpillars, Cockroaches,
Crickets, Cutworms, Earwigs,
Slugs, Snails, Springtails and
Sowbugs prefer freshy textured,
soft-tissued plants and young
growth.
Aphids prefer plants living in a cool
environment. Cockroaches prefer
plants in a warm, humid
environment.
Soil pests (such as Symphylans,
Springtails) prefer to live in soil
having a high percentage of humus
and peat moss.

59

ANTS

Ants do not initiate attacks on most house plants; they are attracted by most dangerous plant pests. But the presence of the industrious ant can only contribute to the damage.

While mealybugs, aphids and scale feast on their favorite flora, they excrete a honeydew-like substance that remains smeared on the infested plant. The substance is a siren song to any ants in the vicinity—and during the spring and summer ants are very often in the vicinity. Ants are so enamored with this substance that they tote its makers—aphids, mealybugs or scale—from plant to plant.

If you find ants crawling about a plant, check first for these other pests. Unsterilized soil often contains ant eggs, and the use of such soil generally explains the presence of ants on a plant not infested by other pests.

While ants do not directly harm adult plants, they may carry off seeds or new seedlings. Whenever they set up house within a planter or large pot their tunnels may disrupt roots.

If you are troubled by ants among your plants, drench the soil of infested plants with a solution of Malathion.

APHIDS

Aphids are a common, serious house plant pest. They have small, soft, light green bodies and an insatiable taste for plant sap. Aphids are generally found clustered around stems and newly budded terminal leaves, and they cause damage by piercing the tender growth and sucking out the rich plant sap.

60

A plant being drained by aphids will lose its vigor. This means that new growth will come in stunted and deformed, leaves may curl and pucker, and the stem may become weak and spindly. The honeydew-like substance they excrete attracts ants and forms a perfect medium for the growth of a destructive sooty black mold.

Tiny white dots on damaged leaves may be the bodies of dead aphids. Young aphids shelter within young leaves, emerging after maturing to search out new leaves and more food.

To get rid of these buggers, rinse an infested plant in warm soapy water. Gently and thoroughly wash all of the foliage, paying special attention to the underside of leaves and new tip ends. Cut off all damaged or badly discolored growth.

Rinse a badly infested plant every six to seven days, and treat the foliage with several applications of a Malathion spray.

If a plant is too damaged to recover, take cuttings of any healthy parts and repot them in pasteurized soil. Spray these parts at least once with Malathion.

CATERPILLARS

Caterpillars are the wormlike immature forms of moths and butterflies. There are many types of caterpillars, and they all share a voracious taste for buds, flowers and leaves. A number of varieties are rapacious enough to strip a plant overnight.

Although you will rarely encounter caterpillars indoors, they may enter a home by clinging to clothes or garden tools, or by hiding in unsterilized soil. Having once settled on a plant, they will conceal themselves during the day by burrowing into the soil or attaching themselves to the undersides of leaves. Most types emerge only at night to feast on a plant's tender parts.

You may notice them curled on leaves, or suspect their presence by the many black specks of excrement-spotted leaves. All too often, the only obvious sign of a caterpillar's presence may be the gaping holes in leaves that appear overnight.

Search the undersides of leaves on a damaged plant for patches of eggs or groupings of small caterpillars. If you find any, cut off and destroy any infested leaves. Examine the plant at night, when larger caterpillars are likely to emerge from the soil or other hiding places to feed. Pick off any you find.

GARDEN CENTIPEDE

(SYMPHYLAN)

Although the symphylan is commonly identified as the "garden centipede," the two critters are not related. True centipedes are generally predators of insects, and not plant pests. You can easily tell the difference between the two. Symphylans have twelve pairs of legs, while centipedes have fifteen pairs; symphylans are blind, while centipedes are sighted; centipedes have poison claws, which they use to paralyze the earthworms, snails and small insects that they prey upon; symphylans do not because they feed only on plants.

Symphylans usually settle in decaying organic matter, such as manure heaps, leaf piles or composted soil. Adults average ¼" long and have white, flattened, wormlike bodies. Light repels them, and they will rarely be discovered on a plant or above its soil surface.

As symphylans are drawn to organic matter, they are most likely to attack ornamental or flowering plants grown in soils having a large percentage of humus or peat moss.

Symphylans are introduced to house plants in unpasteurized soil. Less often, they may be carried into a house on clothing or garden tools. Once settled in a plant's soil, they will grope along root systems, feeding on young roots, root hairs or the submerged section of a plant's stem. An infested plant will stop growing, wilt and even die. Its damaged roots can no longer absorb the nutrients necessary for plant growth and health.

Because symphylans are so rarely seen, you may be at a loss to explain a plant's rapid failure. If you can find no other cause for the damage, turn the plant out and examine its roots. You may notice the small white bugs desperately burrowing back into the soil. If they are present, the roots will appear chewed and perhaps misshapen.

Cut off the damaged roots. Gently wash all of the old soil off the plant, and repot it in pasteurized soil. Dispose of *all* of the old soil.

Symphylans may also be eradicated by treating a plant's soil with a solution of Malathion.

If a plant has been fatally injured, take cuttings of any healthy parts and repot them in pasteurized soil.

COCKROACHES

Cockroaches are too familiar to require description. Dark brown and beetlelike in appearence, they are especially active in damp weather. Once inside a house they will feed on garbage, paper, any food within their reach and, quite often, on the leaves of house plants.

As cockroaches are attracted to moisture, they will most likely attack plants requiring high humidity levels. They may even climb into terrariums.

Cockroaches leave foliage and plant parts badly chewed and raveled. You can use a Malathion spray either on injured plants to stop and attack, or on uninjured plants to prevent an infestation. Household insecticides can be used—as long as you do *not* spray plant foliage.

Because roaches are drawn to decaying material, be sure to keep plant work and display areas free of discarded soil of dead leaves.

CRICKETS

Crickets are related to the grasshopper family, and they are distinguished from their kin by the sound a male cricket produces when he rubs specially designed parts of his front wings together. Some types of crickets are helpful garden predators. Others, most famously the "Mormon cricket," have a disastrous effect on grain crops, fruits and plants.

Field crickets are the most common species, and they *do* have an appetite for vegetables and the foliage, flowers or seeds of plants.

Crickets rarely trouble house plants, but an occasional cricket may inadvertently hop into your lodgings—and it just might discover your plants. If it does, you will find new leaves disappearing overnight. During the day a cricket (or, less often, crickets) will hide under pot saucers, in a house plant's soil, under counters or furniture, or beneath baseboards—in fact, almost any small, dark space.

If you suspect cricket trouble, search the area around your plants. Crickets, like most house plant pests, are drawn to piles of organic material. *Keep plant areas clean.*

Dispose of any crickets you catch on one of your plants. If the problem persists, drench the soil with a solution of Malathion.

Systemic pesticides are often touted as providing effective, long lasting relief from many plant pests, including crickets. However, I do not recommend them.

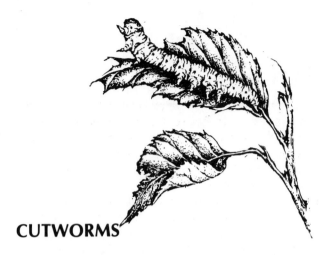

CUTWORMS

Cutworms are a particularly destructive form of moth larvae. They occur in most of the temperate regions of the world, and where present, they attack most forms of plant life.

They have acquired their name through their appearance and feeding habits. Cutworm eggs are attached to blades of grass or weeds. When they hatch, the larvae quickly burrow into the ground. As cutworms grow they acquire a strong resemblance to other worms, having large, soft smooth bodies. They settle in the soil around plants, and emerge at night to feed.

Cutworms often feed by slashing through the stem of young plants just above the soil line. The plant may collapse, or remain upright; but even if it stays upright, the plant cannot long survive with a badly damaged stem. Cutworms may also slice away flower heads or branches on larger plants, and some species crawl along a plant to feed on its leaves or flowers. They tear large, irregular portions out of leaves, working inward from the margins.

A plant may recover from the loss of foliage or flowers, but it cannot recuperate from the partial destruction of its stem.

Cutworms are rarely found indoors. They may be introduced to a plant as eggs or larvae hidden in unpasteurized soil. Or a few may be carried into a home on gardening clothing or tools.

If one of your plants has already suffered a slashed stem, you cannot save it. But if only flowers or branches have been lopped off, you can often save the plant. Stir up the soil, and pick out any cutworms you find. You will find them quite near the soil surface, somnolent as they digest their last meal. Check a plant during the night, and pick off any you find inching along leaves.

A solution of Malathion, applied to the soil, should finish off any infestation. While Diazinon is also recommended as an efficient cutworm poison, it is better used outdoors.

Take cuttings from a badly damaged plant, and repot them in pasteurized soil.

64

EARTHWORMS

The earthworm is one of the most beneficial of creatures, coveted by outdoor gardeners for its continuous ventilation and enrichment of the soil. The tunnels it chews through the earth serve as a primitive but effective ventilating system, allowing oxygen and water to thoroughly permeate the soil. Earthworms swallow quantities of soil, extract its food value, and excrete the remainder as worm casts. These casts, due to the worm's digestive procedure, are rich in nitrates, phosphorus, calcium and potassium—the most important chemical elements for plant health. The fertility of all soil, even depleted ground, is greatly increased by the action of earthworms.

However, they have no business in the small world of a flowerpot. They may clog up the pot's discharge hole or, frustrated by the restrictions of the pot walls, burrow winding tunnels that damage a plant's root system and disturb the necessary processes of plant growth.

Earthworms are nocturnal travelers above ground, so check a plant during the night if you suspect their presence. A very heavy watering will flood burrows and drive the worms to the surface. Lift off any you find and, as a favor to Mother Earth, return them to their proper environment. If the problem persists, turn the plant out and sift through the soil to locate any reluctant worms. Examine the roots for damage and repot the plant in pasteurized soil.

Always inspect house plants you've had—no matter how briefly—outdoors. Check garden tools before you bring them inside. Earthworms have more work than they can handle outdoors, so don't provide an opportunity for them to shirk their profession, eh?

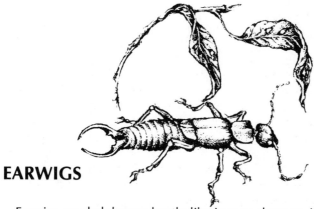

EARWIGS

Earwigs are dark brown beetle-like insects about an inch long. They are readily identified by a tail appendage resembling a tiny pair of forceps. Earwigs are nocturnal feeders, and will attack stems,

65

leaves, flowers and ripening fruit. They occasionally supplement their diet by eating small insects.

Earwigs occur most often in coastal states. They enter houses concealed in clothing left outside to dry, within cut flowers or hidden in other materials. Once inside, they become a terrific nuisance. During the day they conceal themselves in or under furniture, in closets or under floorboards. At night they emerge to scrounge food, and your house plants will be a welcome additon to their diet.

It is said that the earwig (Ferficula auricularia Linnaeus) was so named because it was erroneously believed to prefer setting up house in a human's inner ear.

If holes appear overnight punched through leaves or blossoms, suspect earwigs. Check at night, and if you should find any on a plant, pick them off and destroy them. Spraying plant foliage with Malathion will end all but the most severe of attacks. If the damage continues, spray regularly with Malathion and check likely earwig shelters around your house.

The chemical Sevin is used to control earwigs outdoors. It should *not* be used indoors. Indeed, if used carelessly outdoors it can be harmful to humans. For many years before the introduction of chemical powders and sprays, a poison bran mash was dished out towards evening in areas frequented by earwigs. And it worked—not only against earwigs, but against other insects, birds, dogs and, sometimes, children.

Considering the fatal equality of too many manmade insecticides, gardeners might be interested in one effective method of earwig control employed before the test tube age. The method shrewdly takes advantage of earwigs' attraction to dry, dark places. Flowerpots, with dry moss pressed to their interiors, and inverted and placed on sticks about the garden. The earwigs will be drawn to the pots as particularly appealing accommodations for a daylight nap. Every morning, collect the pots and empty the earwigs into a small container of kerosene. Of course, you needn't use flowerpots—any dry container will do as well. I've even heard of one organic gardener who uses match boxes. The idea is at least a century old—perhaps much older.

Brainy fellows, our forefathers.

FUNGUS GNATS

Fungus gnats are the familiar gray or sooty black dots often seen hovering around house plants. While the adult gnats are harmless—although unattractive—they do lay eggs on the soil

66

surface. These eggs hatch into tiny burrowing white maggots, which feed on a plant's root tissue and root hairs. Large roots may be badly scarred, while small roots may be entirely consumed.

Plants attacked by these maggots will wilt, their leaves will yellow and growth will slow down noticeably. When that happens, the damaged roots are particularly vulnerable to root rot and other diseases.

The presence of adult gnats should indicate the problem you face. You can get rid of the adults by spraying with an aerosol that *specifies* it is safe to use around plants. Immerse an infested plant in clear, lukewarm water to just above the soil line, and allow it to soak overnight. Most of the maggots will be drowned. Because gnats produce new generations every few weeks, continue the water greatment each time you notice a cloud of adults; the gnats will gradually be exterminated.

Malathion applied as a liquid to the soil is also effective in controlling this pest.

Gnats prefer to breed in decaying organic matter, so they most frequently attack plants having soil with a concentration of humus or peat moss. They also enjoy moist environments, so unless you have a plant requiring frequent, heavy waterings, an attack of fungus gnats may be an indication that you've been overwatering.

LEAFMINERS

Leafminers rarely attack house plants, but when they do attack they cause extensive damage. They are the larval form of a number of flies, sawflies and moths.

Leafminers burrow into a leaf and, once safely wedged between its surfaces, they proceed to chew away its interior. Their feeding produced a characteristic "mined" effect on the leaf surface, as the larvae eat tunnels through the leaf.

The Chrysanthemum leafminer chews irregular tunnels that are much lighter than the surrounding leaf color, and speckled with patches of black excrement. Badly damaged leaves shrivel and droop. Leaves of plants infested with the Arborvitae leafminer turn

67

yellow, then a wasted brown. The Azalea leafminers combine several nasty habits. They mine a leaf, causing blisters to appear, and then emerge to roll themselves up into the leaf. After that, they spin their cocoons within the curled leaf.

You cannot mistake a leafminer for any other pest: its damage is distinctive. They are difficult to control because they do their worst damage while they are safely ensconced within a leaf.

Cut off any leaves exhibiting tunnels or discoloration. Also destroy any curled leaves that, when unrolled, reveal leafminers or their cocoons. Allow the soil surface to thoroughly dry out before watering, as the larvae prefer moist plants. Spray an infested plant's foliage with Malathion or rotenone, and soak the soil with a solution of Malathion.

LEAFROLLERS

Leafrollers are small caterpillars, the larval from of several types of moths. Leafrollers feed on leaves that they have carefully rolled around their bodies.

The Rose leaf tier is the form most likely to infest house plants. Its body is pale green, while its head is black. The Rose leaf tier mines the interior of a leaf, then emerges and rolls one or several leaves around itself to form a protected area. The Omnivorous leafroller is yellow brown, and both the Rose leaf and Omnivorous leafrollers feed on flowers, leaves, vegetables, trees, fruits and shrubs.

Leafrollers hatch out of distinctive egg bundles. The eggs producing the Rose leaf tier appear as overlapping green bulges attached to a plant's branches. The eggs of the Omnivorous leafroller are green, and resemble flattened droplets shingled one over the other.

If you do not notice egg bundles, you will probably notice the distinctively rolled leaves. Pick off and destroy any infested leaves. Spray Malathion on the foliage.

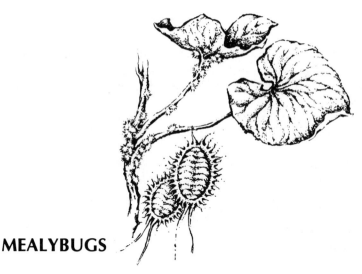

MEALYBUGS

Mealybugs are stubborn, destructive and painfully common house plant pest. These tiny insects form white powdery masses on leaf axils or along stem joints. They have oval, soft, segmented bodies covered by layers of a white, wax-like substance. The females are very prolific, laying three hundred to six hundred eggs at a time in a small waxy hump. The eggs hatch into light-colored smooth-bodied nymphs. Both nymphs and adults feed by inserting sharp beaks into plant tissue and sucking the sap out.

You may notice cotton-like masses seemingly tucked onto the plant, or you may suddenly find ants moving about the soil surface. Mealybugs excrete a honeydew-like substance that attracts ants and, as if that were not enough, also provides an excellent medium for the growth of a sooty-colored mold. A plant suffering a mealybug attack will wilt, growth will cease or continue irregularly, and large numbers of leaves will drop off. Left untreated, mealybugs can rapidly kill a plant.

You can scrape many of the bugs off, but you are certain to miss some. And just one female can repopulate a mealybug colony in short order. A much-cited remedy calls for dabbing each bug with a cotton swab dipped in alcohol. The alcohol penetrates the bug's waxy armor and quickly kills it. However, this is a tedious process, you will probably miss some of the bugs, and the alcohol can damage plant tissue.

A better remedy is to spray plant foliage with Malathion. But be sure to pick as many of the bugs off as you can reach before you spray. Spray again after several days.

Malathion however, damages some ferns. If you have a fern under mealybug attack, pick off as many of the pests as you can and apply systematic granules to the soil. The granules will take several days to end the infestation, but they do work.

The Citrus mealybug is one of the commonest—and most deadly—of the mealybug tribe. The Longtailed mealybug, named by the two filaments equal to its body length it carries behind it, is a frequent visitor on avocado plants.

The Ground mealybug feeds on the roots of plants, especially cacti. If you discover it clustered around a plant's roots, repot the plant and treat the soil with a solution of Malathion or systemic granules.

Keep an especially close eye on your cacti, as many species of the plant have bunting similar in appearance to a clan of mealybugs. If a cactus having such bunting starts to fail, or if the bunting seems to suddenly expand, you may have mealybugs. Pick off any bugs you find, and treat the plant with systemic granules.

MILLIPEDES

Although often called the "thousand legged" insect, millipedes in fact have only thirty to forty pairs of legs. They also have hard shelled, cylindrical, many-segmented bodies and short, segmented antennae. They average an inch in length. Most species are brown, although some are tinged with pink, and a few species are entirely gray.

Millipedes can be found outdoors coiled in rich soil, or scaverging from piles of organic wastes. When disturbed, they can move quite rapidly, presenting a dizzy prospect of legs. Some millipedes prey on smaller garden insects, but most of them carry away seeds, attack young roots and slash through the stems of seedlings. The insects they eat are plant pests, making them of some small help outdoors. But indoors, deprived of that predatory role, they are simply destructive.

Millipedes are infrequent house plant pests. An occasional individual may be carried into the house on tools or clothing or, as some species are troublesome to greenhouse growers, a few may enter hidden in a plant's soil. A serious infestation is rare.

Fortunately, they can be easily located. If you find seeds missing, new roots disturbed or seedlings slashed, suspect millipedes. During the day they will conceal themselves in any dark areas around plants. Also check the soil of any damaged plants, as the humus or peat moss might have proved irresistible to a millipede. They prefer damp conditions, so check any plants that normally require frequent waterings for signs of millipede damage. Remove and destroy any insects your search turns up.

If you cannot locate the millipedes, and damage persists, treat the soil of vulnerable or damaged plants with a solution of Malathion.

70

NEMATODES

Nematodes are an especially difficult problem. Some botanists and plant pathologists calssify them as a disease, while others insist they be considered a pest. The disagreement centers over the decision as to whether the bugs damage plants, or simply serve to introduce diseases to the root system.

House plant owners can avoid this thorny problem of nematodes by using only sterilized soil.

There is, however, the chance that someone may have sold you an infected plant. Sadly, you probably won't know until it's too late.

Nematodes are microscopic worms. They settle in root systems, and one way or another, they cause trouble. Infected roots develop galls, or knots, shrinking or becoming grotesquely distorted. Growth will slow, then stop, and foliage will wilt and drop off. Secondary infections will enter the plant through its damaged and near-dead roots. Then the plant quickly dies.

If one of your plants begins to fail, examine the roots. If the roots appear badly damaged, my suggestion is to destroy the plant and discard its soil. Scour everything that has come into contact with the plant, including your tools, clothes and work or display areas. Do not touch any other plants until you have scrubbed your hands. Nematodes are terrifically infectious.

The preparation V-C 13 is said to be of some help in combating nematodes. Nematocides are chemicals formulated for use against this destructive problem. However, they are primarily intended for use outdoors.

I have heard of, but cannot vouch for, a home-brewed remedy that calls for soaking an infested plant for two hours in a solution composed of one teaspoon of chlorine bleach to one quart of water. The liquid should come to just above the soil surface. Harsh detergents are no good for plants, but if you are desperate, you might consider this treatment. Although I have heard some swear by it, I have never found it to work.

Nematodes are a costly, disruptive problem responsible for wide-scale injury to crops and plants. If you use pasteurized soil, you should never have to worry about their presence. If nematodes arrive at your house hidden in some plant's soil, my suggestion is to destroy the plant. Nematodes infect plants rapidly, and it is far, far better to lose one plant than to lose an entire collection.

SCALE

Scale can destroy a plant without your ever being able to identify the cause. These tiny insects appear to be nothing more than the normal knobs and protuberances of a plant stem. They suck vital juices out a plant, causing leaves to spot, turn yellow and fall off. The entire plant may wilt, and the plant's growth rate will take a nosedive.

Scale are a common house plant problem, so you should be on the lookout for them. If you notice any new knobs on stems, or any tiny domes attached to the underside of leaves, probe them with a fingernail. Scale shells have a waxy texture. They may feel quite soft as you probe them, and they can easily be scraped off with a gentle motion.

Scale also excrete a sticky honeydew-like substance that attracts ants, and provides a medium for the growth of some fungus diseases. If you find ants crawling about a plant, search for scale. And get rid of the ants, for all too often they act as cheerful insect Typhoid Marys, giving the scale a piggyback ride from plant to plant.

You can end a mild scale attack by hand-picking them off a plant. Or you can wash an infested plant in warm soapy (not detergent) water. Gently, but firmly, run your fingers over the stem and leaves, taking care to wash the entire plant. The scale should readily drop off. Rinse the plant, and repeat the process once or twice a week until the plant has regained its vitality.

Malathion can be sprayed on plant foliage to halt an attack. As ferns cannot abide most chemical sprays, pick off any scale you find on a fern, and treat the soil with systemic granules.

Plants that suffer repeated scale attacks may be sprayed in the early spring with a petroleum oil spray. As with all plant preparations, read the label to determine upon which plants it can safely be used.

72

SNAILS, SLUGS

Snails and slugs are familiar inhabitants of most outdoor gardens. They are not insects, but land-dwelling mollusks belonging to the same family as oysters, clams and other shellfish.

Snails have soft, unsegmented bodies protected by hard, humped shells. When disturbed, they will completely withdraw into their stout homes. Slugs are shelless snails. Both snails and slugs are dark brown, gray or black in appearance.

While there are thirty species of slugs and some two hundred species of snails, only a few types are garden pests. Those types are generally nocturnal feeders. They feast on plants by rasping holes in leaves with their sharp mouth parts. While the pierced leaves may not furnish sufficient evidence to identify the pest, both slugs and snails leave characteristically slimy trails. Your problem will most probably be limited to a few individuals carried in on garden tools or clothes. They present a rare and easily controlled problem.

If you find leaf damage and slimy tracings, search under pot saucers and in dark areas around your plants. Snails, and especially the fat, defenseless slugs, carefully conceal themselves during the day. Remove any that you find. If you cannot locate them (and they *have* had a good deal more practice at hiding than you have had at looking), check again during the night when they should be out and feeding.

You may have heard of a home-fashioned remedy that calls for sinking a jar lid of beer (stale or fresh) or fermented grape juice into the soil surface of a previously attacked plant. Slugs and snails—like most insects—are creatures of habit, and they will often return to a plant they have already attacked. A snail or slugs will be drawn to the brew, they will attempt to sample it, they will fall in and, yes, they will drown. I have been assured by sober plant owners that the remedy works.

Slugs will be discouraged by sharp pebbles, bits of crockery or shards of brick placed around a pot's base. They avoid anything that bruises their unprotected flesh.

Various baits, traps or chemicals are available to kill snails and slugs, and all of them are based on the potent Metaldehyde mixture. They are effective, but dangerous to you if used improperly. Such chemicals are really intended for outdoor use.

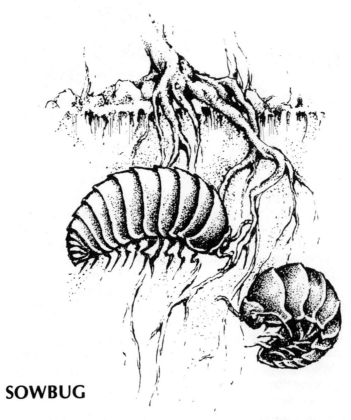

SOWBUG

Sowbug is the name given to several similar soil pests. They are really not bugs at all, but tiny relatives of the crayfish and other crustaceans. They have flat, oval bodies, are commonly brown, have seven pairs of legs and grow to an average length of ½". One species—the pillbug—curls itself into a pill-like ball whenever it is threatened.

Sowbugs have gills, and, quite naturally, they prefer a damp environment. Once they have been inadvertently carried into a house, or have somehow found their way in, they may be attracted to plants. You may find them in the saucers placed beneath flowerpots to collect water run-off. Or they may settle into clumps of decaying organic matter.

Young sowbugs will devour young roots, stems and seedlings. Seedlings will die, and mature plants attacked by sowbugs will wilt. Leaves will droop and lose their color, as the roots may no longer be functioning properly. While such symptoms are too general to be of much help, check for sowbugs when you investigate the problem.

Cacti are frequent sowbug targets, and you may discover the bugs gathered in numbers of the plant's crown or along the rim of its pot.

If you find any sowbugs, pick them off and dispose of them. Use a Malathion spray on the soil surface to kill or repel the pest.

74

SPIDER MITES

Spider mites have an average length of ¹/₅₀th of an inch, and are next to invisible on a plant. Often only the closest of inspections will reveal their presence. Their size, their rapid proliferation and their great thirst for plant sap make them of the most difficult—and deadliest—of house plant pests.

Spider mites are not true insects. They belong to the class Arachnida, and are thus related to spiders, scorpions and ticks. When examined under a magnifying glass, they can be seen to differ noticeably from most insects. Spider mites have four pairs of legs, while insects have three pairs. Unlike insects, spider mites have no antennae. Their small, round bodies are unsegmented, while insects have bodies divided into several segments (think of the ant, for instance).

Because a mite is not often a visible pest, you must learn to recognize the symptoms of a mite infestation. You should examine all of your plants regularly, and when you do, check for any tiny webbing spun across the underside of a leaf, tied on a terminal leaf or thrown across a leaf axil. The webs have a coarse, mealy texture.

Spider mites push their sucking mouth parts into tender leaf tissue and draw the sap out. As leaves are drained they become mottled. Gray patches dot the leaf surface, producing a noticeable stippled effect. It might almost seem as if the leaves have been painted by applying drops of gray and green paint. Leaves also lose their sheen. Once a leaf has lost its color, it can never regain it. But it need not fall off, if the mites are eradicated. If the mites are not stopped, the plant may become defoliated. Certainly foliage will droop, the plant will cease growing, and it might fail.

Isolate a plant as soon as you even suspect a mite attack. They are very, *very* contagious. Scour your tools and your plant work and display areas, and scrub your hands before touching healthy plants.

Hold an infested plant under a strong steam of lukewarm water and make certain that the water runs thoroughly over the foliage. The constant force of the water will carry away all of the webbing as well as most of the mites. Repeat the procedure once every two days for a

75

week to eliminate any stubborn survivors. Keep the plant in isolation for at least another week, just in case there are any mites still alive. They *are* stubborn pests.

Ced-O-Flora, a spray composed of petroleum, soap, and cedar and hemlock oils, is reputed to be effective against mites. Three teaspoons of the mix should be used for each pint of water. Spray an infested plant's foliage at weekly intervals, taking pains to cover the underside of leaves and all leaf axils.

There are a number of preparations intended for exclusive use against this destructive, common pest. Some chemicals, notably the systemic sprays, are very strong, and should be used with great caution. Ovex and Tedion are miticides that are said to be effective against mites, but quite harmless to other living things. Any rotenone-based aerosol spray may also be of some help in ending an attack.

The Two-Spotted mite is a most familiar form of the mites to attack house plants. Its tiny oval body is yellow and green. Two dark spots appear prominently on its back—that is, prominently under a magnifying glass.

Broad mites restrict themselves to a diet of cyclamen, African violet, begonias, fuchsia, lantana, and geranium leaves. Their pale bodies are smaller than those of other mites, but broader across the middle. Their attacks cause blisters to pop out on leaves. The leaves may also become brittle, discolor, or fade to a limp paleness. They will ultimately pucker and droop.

The Cyclamen mite is named for its preference in plants. It will suck foliage until numbers of leaves become wrinkled, discolored and noticeably coarsened.

The camp followers of a mite attack include chlorosis, bacteria and fungus infections.

Kelthane is often recommended for the elimination of Broad and Cyclamen mites.

All plant mites are prolific, voracious pests. If you do not discover an infestation until much damage has been done, it may be best to get rid of the plant. Badly damaged plants are hard to bring around, and if you live in cramped quarters, the chance of one plant infecting many is rather high.

SPRINGTAILS

Springtails are tiny wingless insects, so named by their use of tail-like appendages to propel themselves through the air. Although there are two thousand species of this primitive bug, only one—the

Garden Springtail—is harmful to plants. It has a round, dark, soft body with yellow markings and a distinct head. Distinct under a magnifying glass, that is, as the bug averages a length of $1/25$th of an inch.

Springtails chew small round holes in leaves, young roots or seedlings. Although they may feed at night, a heavy watering will drive them to the soil surface, where they will appear as small stabs of color (bright brown or black) leaping about in a startling and most agitated manner.

They are not a serious problem, but their presence may indicate that you have been giving a plant too much water (as they find damp conditions especially attractive). Moderate your watering habits, giving as much water, but less frequently.

You can float the springtails out by soaking an infested plant in clear water that reaches to just above the soil line. Let the plant soak for several hours. Allow it to begin to dry, and apply a solution of Malathion to eliminate any stubborn hold-outs.

THRIPS

Thrips cause more trouble then their size might warrant. So small and slender, they can be perceived only as dark moving objects on a plant. Nevertheless, thrips can accomplish a good deal of damage without your suspecting their presence.

Thrips will leave a plant speckeled with tiny dark blobs of excrement. Their rasping mouth parts scar leaves, creating pockmarks and whitened scars on the undersides of leaves. Flower buds may drop off. Leaves acquire a papery texture and develop blisters wherever female thrips insert their eggs.

Washing a plant thoroughly with lukewarm soapy water will destroy most infestations. Malathion, sprayed at regular intervals for one or two weeks, will clear away any survivors and eliminate new generations.

WHITE FLY

White flies are small insects that resemble moths much more than flies. These tiny white pests may go unnoticed until the plant is disturbed, and, to your astonishment, white clouds will billow out of the plant and hover over it. Or, even more disturbing, they may push off in search of another plant.

White flies mass on the undersides of leaves, piercing them to suck sap out of the plant. The nymphs, or larvae, are especially voracious feeders. Leaves will yellow, wilt and fall off; then the entire plant weakens and seems to slump in exhaustion. At one point in their maturation, the flies excrete a sticky substance that forms a medium for the growth of molds.

If any of these symptoms appear on a plant, you can verify your diagnosis by gently stirring the foliage. If white fly are present, an agitated swarm will spring off the plant into the air.

While on the plant, they are difficult to reach, as they huddle far back on the underside of leaves. And their rapid multiplication makes it impossible to clear a plant of them quickly.

Wash the plant with warm soapy water, scrubbing thoroughly and gently along the underside of leaves. Rinse the plant, and then spray the foliage with Malathion. Repeat the process several times over a span of two to three weeks, spraying with Malathion after each plant bath.

A systemic solution may be applied to the soil, or placed on it in the form of systemic granules.

A word of caution: white flies produce a new generation every five days, and after two to three weeks, they may become immune to the treatment. Switch to another preparation, and continue the treatment.

Isolate a plant as soon as you even *suspect* white flies. Lantana and fuchsia seem to be almost perpetual hosts to the pest and, if you have been repeatedly troubled, you might do better by eliminating these plants from your collection. White flies are such a nasty, stubborn problem that I would recommend doing anything to avoid an infestation.

Research is now being conducted on ways to control the white fly. Until they figure something out, hang in there.

CHEMICAL WARFARE

I do not like to use insecticides. I do not like to but, unfortunately, often I have no choice. Some pests are *so* stubborn and *so* damaging to plants that nothing less than a poison will effectively remove them.

Throughout this chapter, I have consistently recommended what I consider to be the mildest of preparations. I have done so because these preparations are the least dangerous to handle, thus avoiding the chance of your being poisoned along with the bugs. And because, in all but a few cases, they are sufficient. Never use a stronger chemical mix than you have to.

When you do apply a pesticide, I strongly urge you to follow the procedure listed below.

First of all: *read the instructions printed on the package–and follow them*. Prepare the preparation as the package suggests, using the exact dose the instructions state—*don't* add an extra smidgeon for added punch. Just, please, do what the manufacturer tells you to do. Too strong a mixture might damage the plant along with clearing out the pests. Don't dose a plant more often than the instructions suggest, or you may be putting yourself in a race with the pests to see who can destroy your plant first.

Do not bend so close as to inhale the vapors of a preparation. If it is a liquid, be careful not to splash any on your skin or clothes. If you are splashed, wash the area immediately with soap and water.

Do not apply any poison while children or animals are near at hand. After applying it, move the convalescent plant high enough to discourage children or pets from investigating.

If you spray a plant, spray it only in a well-ventilated area.

If it is a liquid preparation, and must be diluted in water, mix only as much as you need. If there is any left over, discard it—do not attempt to store it. And *don't* pour it down the kitchen sink.

Store cans and jars well away from any prying hands or paws. If you have small children, store the mixtures in a cabinet they cannot reach, or put a padlock on a cabinet they can reach. If any of the preparations are aerosol sprays, store them away from heat or sunlight as well as children and animals.

Follow to the letter all directions printed on the preparations you use.

What kinds of pesticides are there?

There are contact poisons, that kill soon after they are applied to an infested plant.

There are stomach poisons, which are applied to foliage. When the pest eats the foliage, it dies.

There are systemics, which are applied to an infested plant's soil. The poison is drawn up into the plant through the roots, and distributed through all its parts. The entire plant becomes poisonous—whenever a pest takes a bite from any portion of the plant, it is swallowing poison. Systemics remain in a plant for several weeks, giving it additional protection.

Drenches are preparations applied to the soil. Most drenches are contact poisons, although some kill as their vapors are diffused through the foliage.

Malathion is the brand name of contact pesticide. It can be sprayed on a plant or applied as a drench to the soil. I have found it to be effective against the attacks of most common house plant pests. I have stressed its use in this chapter, not only because of its effectiveness, but because it is relatively non-toxic to mammals (mammals like you, your children and your pets). However, it is not effective against all pests, and it can be harmful to some plants, such as ferns. Read the label to determine if it is safe to use on the plant you had in mind, and please obey all the instructions and warnings.

Fungicides are also contact poisons. They can be purchased as liquids or powders, and they are intended for use against plant disease organisms. Bordeaux mixture, Captan, Ferbam and Maneb are all brand names of fungicides.

Miticides are contact insecticides intended for use only against spider mites. Generally, they should not be applied to edible plants. Follow directions carefully—remember, no matter *how* safe a pesticide or miticide is supposed to be, it is a *poison*. So take precautions, yes? Dimite and Tedion are brand names of miticides.

Nicotine sulfate can be used as a soil drench or spray intended for use against foliage insects. Be very careful not to inhale this powder as you are mixing it in water, for it can be quite toxic.

Rotenone is a contact insecticide available as an aerosol spray. It is said to be quite safe, being non-toxic to mammals. But that *doesn't* mean you should develop a heavy trigger finger.

Ced-O-Flora is a liquid concentrate made of petroleum products, soap and oils. It is supposed to be effective in controlling scale and mealybug attacks.

Systemics are available as liquid concentrates or powders. Although they are lethally effective, I do not recommend them, except in extreme cases. They are simply *too* strong, and in my opinion, too dangerous for household use. Remember that they permeate every portion of a plant—and they linger on. What happens when you routinely handle that plant—a plant that may look, and is, quite healthy, and yet quite poisonous? Or what happens when a child, or a pet, chews on a leaf plucked from that plant? No, you don't need that risk. There are other, less toxic preparations that generally do the job. I suggest that you use them.

80

How do you apply these preparations?

Many mixes are available as liquid concentrates, and can be used as either a spray or soil drench.

To use as a spray, dilute a preparation with water according to the instructions printed on the package. Pour the liquid into a hand-held sprayer, and apply a fine mist to plant leaves and leaf axils. Make sure that the spray is applied to the underside of leaves, since they are a frequent refuge for pests.

A drench is prepared from a liquid concentrate or a powder dissolved in water. Use a watering can to pour the required amount of liquid onto the soil. Wash the can out thoroughly, or, better yet, reserve it for just such a purpose for future treatments.

Aerosol sprays are the most inexact of treatments. They are also often the weakest. I do not recommend aerosol sprays, unless you have infrequent, mild infestations. In that case, they will be adequate. But if the problem is more serious, you will do better to prepare the poison yourself.

Again:

Spray only in well ventilated areas.

Always use the mildest poison applicable to the specific problem.

Do not inhale the fumes given off by any of these mixes.

If you spill or spray any on yourself, wash it off with hot water and soap *immediately*.

And please, please keep all chemicals away from your children and pets.

And when you use pesticides, use them sparingly. I do not recommend regular applications of a poison to forestall trouble. You are only risking much greater trouble.

Never use chemicals when a non-chemical treatment is available and has been recommended as being effective.

When you use a chemical, use the mildest available for your specific problem. *Don't* roll out the big guns when a small caliber will do.

Many types of insects can be hand picked off a plant. Some infestations can be ended by scrubbing a plant with soapy water. Other non-chemical methods prove equally effective in ending infestations. Many of these methods have been described in this chapter, and I would like to encourage you to try them—or any others you might learn—when the need arises.

Chemicals should be your last, not your first, line of defense. There will be times when you will need them, and I cannot deny that using them is better than losing a plant. Just don't let their use become a reflex action—don't reach for the aerosol each time you see a bug.

The effects of chemicals on our environment, and on our bodies, are hotly debated now. Until the evidence is in, I can only urge you to expose yourself to as little additional risk as possible. Chemicals are a part of plant doctoring—but they are far from being the whole of it. Like the wise doctor you are, use them only as you must.

Chapter 14.

House Plant Diseases

Injuries or imbalanced environments weaken plants and make them vulnerable to infections of fungus or bacteria. Excessively high humidity, temperatures above 75° or below 55°, overwatering, insufficient light, and pollution all damage a plant, and provide opportunities for infection.

Fungus infections are the most common house plant diseases. A fungus can rot plant tissue, turning it soft and pulpy; it can turn leaves brown or yellow, or mark them with spots, bands or depressions: it will disrupt vital plant processes. Untreated, a fungus infection can kill a plant.

Fortunately, if you follow the procedures for plant care, a disease may never have an opportunity to strike. If it does, some surgery, combined with post-operative care and a fungicide, can save most plants suffering from a disease.

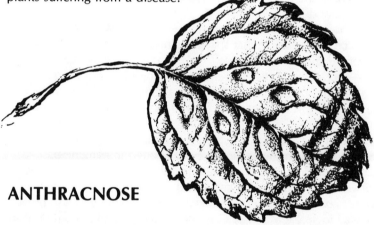

ANTHRACNOSE

Anthracnose is a fungus infection whose chief identifying factor is depressed spots on leaf surfaces. These sunken spots have dark rims and dry, dark centers. Leaf tips may shrivel and turn brown. Leaves may be banded by dark stripes.

Oleander is particularly susceptible to anthracnose. The spots on oleander leaves have whitish centers and dark brown or black rims.

Rubber plants are also quite vulnerable. Infected leaves develop bad burns on leaf tips, while the leaf margins turn yellow. Pale swellings may occur along leaf veins.

Anthracnose seems to attack a plant suffering from chronic overwatering. Water an infected plant only enough to keep it from badly wilting. Remove all discolored, damaged leaves. Foliar fungicides, such as Maneb or Zineb, may be sprayed on healthy foliage to prevent the spread of the infection.

BOTRYTIS

Botrytis is a grayish-white growth appearing on the upper leaves of African violet plants. It is a fungus, said to be caused by plants receiving inadequate ventilation. It may also occur when several African violets have been jammed together in a space too small to accommodate them.

It is a virulent fungus and is terribly contagious, so isolate a plant as soon as you discover the pale, moldy growth. As no sure cure exists and recovery is uncertain, I would suggest discarding any plants having botrytis on a number of leaves. Concentrate your efforts on plants having less than a half-dozen infected leaves.

Remove any leaves spotted by the fungus. Give a plant a location normally receiving plenty of diffused sunlight. Give the plant good ventilation, without exposing it to drafts. Don't spray or mist the leaves. Water the plant from the bottom up *only* (See chapter 8, WATER). Good luck.

Keep the plant isolated for several weeks. If no white growth appears on the leaves in that space of time, return the plant to its accustomed spot.

Give your plants sufficient ventilation. Don't let your rooms become stuffy, or constantly filled with cigarette smoke, cooking fumes or stale air. It is not good for you, and it is positively bad for your plants.

And don't shove plants together. If you lack space, use your ingenuity. Buy plant racks, or use plants potted in hanging baskets. Whatever you do, don't cram them together in the mistaken belief that it won't hurt. Crowding can retard growth or cause uneven growth, as only parts of a plant are exposed to sunlight; it also proves a fast way to spread disease. Give them space—plants should not so overlap that their branches become intermingled.

CHLOROSIS

Chlorosis is a noncontagious deficiency disease occurring in plants potted in an excessively alkaline soil. Although plants need some alkalinity in the soil, too much interferes with the absorption of iron and trace elements necessary for plant health.

A chlorotic plant will have yellow leaves. Leaf veins may remain green, providing a startling contrast. Or, leaf ends may whiten or turn brown. The growth rate will decline, and new leaves may grow in malformed.

84

You could remedy the problem by applying "chelated" iron to the soil. But the plant may be lacking in trace elements, as well as iron. Use an acid-rich plant food, and test the soil with a pH kit to determine if the imbalance has been corrected.

(See chapter 5 for further information on soil pH, acid and alkaline soil, and nutritional problems.)

crown + stem rot

CROWN AND STEM ROT

Zealous overwatering, excessive humidity and very high or low temperature levels encourage the growth of several types of fungus on house plants. These fungi cause plant tissue along the crown and stems to rot, turning soft and pulpy to the touch.

Cut out all rotted tissue, and dust the incision with a plant fungicide (such as Captan or Ferbam). While the plant is recuperating, water it less frequently.

If you suspect that you have regularly watered too often, be more judicious in the future.

If the humidity level is uncomfortably high, you can bring it down by providing additional ventilation for the room. Open a door, open all the windows, or bring in a fan. Just don't let a draft blow directly over the injured plant.

And remember that most plants prefer temperatures between 75° and 55° F.

The most frequent cause of rot is overwatering. So don't get overzealous with that watering can!

DAMPING-OFF DISEASE

Damping-off disease is a fungus present in unpasteurized soil. It mainly attacks seedlings, destroying young root and stem tissue and causing the apprentice plant to lean woefully towards the ground. An infected seedling will die in a day.

You should never lose a seedling to damping-off *if you pot on pasteurized soil*. If a seedling looks wobbly, or if it begins to wilt, reduce the amount of humidity, lower the temperature and water the seedling sparingly. Dust any seedlings you suspect are infected with a fungicide.

If you are anxious for the health of your seedlings, keep in mind that the disease occurs most frequently during very hot weather.

LEAF SPOTS

Leaf spots are a symptom of a bacterial or fungal infection. The infection occurs because the plant has been treated improperly, having received either too much or too little of some vital element.

The spots generally have yellow margins, while the centers of spots are white, brown or black. Badly spotted leaves often fall off.

Remove all infected leaves, and treat the remaining foliage with a foliar fungicide.

86

Overwatering, inadequate light, insufficient ventilation and excessive humidity weaken a plant and make it vulnerable to infection. To avoid this problem, increase the amount of light you are giving a plant, improve ventilation around the plant, and water less frequently, allowing the soil surface to dry out between waterings.

Leaf spots are a sign that you have been doing something wrong. Review your care of the plant, refer back to earlier chapters for a summary of the basics, and correct your mistake.

MILDEWS

Mildews occur on plants growing in very damp environments. Mildews are parasitic organisms that coat leaves with a gray downy substance. The growth obstructs light, and may cause leaves to wither, curl up and die.

Remove all infected leaves, and lower the humidity, and ventilate the plant area. If the problem persists, spray the leaves with a foliar fungicide.

MOLDS

Mold is a term loosely used to describe a variety of fungus infections. Only two types of "mold" commonly occur on house plants.

Aphids, scale and mealybugs excrete a honeydew-like substance while they are feeding on the juices of a house plant. Under humid conditions, the sticky droplets form a medium for the growth of a sooty black mold. While the mold is not directly harmful, it does obstruct a leaf'f absorption of light, and it is unsightly.

A pasty white or grayish mold springing up on the soil surface is a sure sign that you have been watering too frequently. Such a mold grows only a soil that is constantly damp—and constantly wet soil may cause rots and damage roots.

Use lukewarm soapy water to wash away sooty molds. Examine the plant to determine which of the three pests is attacking it, and apply the suggested fungicide.

Scrape off as much of the grayish soil mold as you can, and mix the remainder of the fungicide thoroughly around and into the soil. Reduce the frequency of your waterings.

ROOT ROT

Roots rot when they are infected by a fungus because infected roots cannot draw in the moisture and nourishment vital to a plant's survival. A plant suffering from root rot may develop a bare stem. Leaves will brown, wilt and fall off. The plant will exhibit all the symptoms of chronic underwatering, and no matter how often you water, symptoms persist.

If you suspect root rot, turn the plant out of its pot. Gently brush away any soil clinging to the roots. If it is root rot, the roots will be discolored, shriveled or pulpy.

Cut the roots back to healthy growth, and dust the new root ends with a fungicide. Re-pot the plant, in a *new* pot, with *sterilized* soil. Water the plant sparingly. If the attack has been severe, drench the soil with a fungicide.

If the roots cannot be salvaged, take cuttings of any healthy growth and pot them in sterilized soil.

A Note on Fungicides

Fungicides are preparations designed to destroy disease organisms. They also serve to prevent the reoccurrence of an infection. Fungicides are available as soluble powders or as concentrated liquids. They may be used to spray foliage, dust plant parts, or drench a plant's soil. Trade names include Bordeaux mixture, Captan, Ferbam, Maneb and Zineb.

Consult the section on chemicals for information on how to prepare and apply fungicides.

PLANTS SENSITIVE TO INFECTION

Most plants are susceptible to infection, given appropriately bad conditions. The plants listed here seem prone to particular infections, especially if they have been injured or mistreated. However, if a plant not listed here develops definite symptoms of disease, it must have that disease and it should be treated accordingly. Remember, most diseases are preventable through proper care.

African Violet—Crown and stem rot, leaf spot, root rot
Aglaonema—Anthracnose, crown and stem rot
Aloe—Root rot

Begonias—Crown and stem rot, root rot

Cacti (and other succulents)—Crown and stem rot, root rot
Citrus—Anthracnose

Dieffenbachia—Crown and stem rot
Dracaenas—Leaf spot

Ficus—Anthracnose, mildew, mold

Geranium—Crown and stem rot, leaf spot
Gloxinia (and other gesneriads)—Crown and stem rot, leaf spot, root rot

Kalanchoe—Anthracnose, root rot

Ligustrum—Leaf spot

Oleander—Anthracnose

Palms—Anthracnose, root rot
Philodendron—Crown and stem rot

Roses—Leaf spot, mildew, mold

Damping-off diseases attack only seedlings. These diseases attack the seedlings of soft-textured plants most frequently.

Mildews and molds often grow on the honeydew-like substance smeared on plant parts by aphids, mealybug and scale. Refer to the list of plants and their pests to verify which plants are attacked, and thus become candidates for a mildew or mold.

Chapter 15
When You Take a Vacation

Your much-needed vacation need not prove fatal to your plants. In winter, when most house plants are dormant, they need only be protected from frost or excessive cold. If it is practical, remove them from windowsills and group them in the center of a room. If you will be away for approximately one week, and if the plants have not been recently watered, give them a modest drink. That should suffice.

For a summer vacation, you must take added precautions. Even if you plan to be gone only a week, your plants will probably need water in your absence. You can, of course, rely upon a friend; but if none volunteer for the job, there are alternatives. You can put the plants requiring water most often in your bathtub. Run cool water into the tub until there is at least 2" of water in that portion of the tub nearest the drain. Because tubs are slanted towards the drain, if you have 2" of water at one end, there will be a little less than 1" at the other, more elevated, end.

I do not recommend this method for any situation less than an emergency, as I suspect that plants having their roots immersed in water for a week or more may begin to rot. But if you have no alternative, do it, placing larger plants in the deep end, and smaller plants in the shallow end. Be certain that the stopper does not leak, or you will come home to a dry tubful of wilted plants.

You can wrap the most sensitive or thirstiest of your plants in plastic bags. Water the plants receiving this treatment thoroughly, then put each pot in a plastic bag and tie the bag around the rim of the pot so that it covers the soil surface loosely. The bag will delay water evaporation. But *don't* place the entire plant in a bag—reserve that process for the treatment of trauma or the correction of a humidity problem.

You can use your ingenuity to devise other methods, and *don't worry*. Your plants may not do as well in your absence, but as long as they have some water, they should get through. And when you return, you can bring them quickly round to their former state of green health by judicious applications of water and some trimming.

. . .AND WHEN YOUR PLANTS TAKE ONE

Some people feel that moving plants outside provides a refreshing change of climate that will revive droopy leaves or restore a healthy green color. I personally feel that this creates more problems than it could solve, but yes, you can move all but the most sensitive of your house plants outdoors for the summer. But do not bring them out until both the days and nights have turned quite temperate, and be sure to bring them back in before the first frost.

You might want to expose them to the outdoors gradually, by keeping them for a day or two on a porch or in some area that has a roof, but is open to the elements. Plants need a day or two to adjust to the variety of conditions outdoors, as they have been used to steady temperatures with little variation.

You might group them together alongside doors or on patios and on walks, on sun decks, along the perimeters of your outdoor garden or along low brick walls. Try not to put them in a position entirely vulnerable to summer winds and rains.

You can even sink house plants in garden soil up to their pot rims. However, when you bring plants out—be forewarned. They will be exposed to varying climatic conditions, and they will encounter a much larger variety of plant pests. So keep a close eye on your plants throughout their vacation.

You may want to apply preventative doses of pesticides to protect your plants. Give them regular applications of fertilizer. Also trim away dead foliage and keep soil surface *clean*. Be sure to water them at least once a week if there has been no noticeable rainfall within the last five days.

Don't bother moving large plants outdoors, or plants displayed in planters—it's just too much trouble. And don't carry rare or very sensitive plants outdoors, unless you have the soul of a gambler.

Some of your plants will do very well outside, growing and shining with green health. Others won't, so bring them back indoors immediately, examine them for pests and infections, and treat any trouble you discover.

Begin moving your plants back indoors by the middle of August, and have them all back inside by the middle of September. *Now* comes the hard part.

Give each returning plant a *thorough* (and I must stress the thorough) examination. Remove any dead growth and any debris that has accumulated on the soil surface. And check the plant—then check it again—for *any* sign of an insect infestation or an infection. Don't put the vacationers right back among their non-traveling companions, but keep any plants that have summered outdoors isolated for at least a week. Then, if no symptoms of trouble develop, move them back to their usual spots. And during that first week, try to keep the temperature of the house below 72°, to give the plants an opportunity to readjust to the conditions indoors.

There is no reason that your plants cannot enjoy a summer communing with nature—as long as you keep a close watch on them and make sure that they receive regular applications of the necessities. Remember, they may be outside but they still depend on you.

Appendix

GROWING PLANTS FROM SEEDS

You can grow many houseplants from seeds, and by doing so you can save yourself a considerable expense. Whether you have five or fifty plants, growing replacements or additions from seeds offers you the opportunity to keep expanding your collection at a very small cost.

What does it take to grow a seed? You need a container for the seeds, and you need a soil mix to plant the seed (or seeds) in. Kits are now available in many garden supply centers that include seeds and sterile potting mix in a plastic or aluminum container. All you need do is add water and watch the seeds grow. Seeds and seedlings must have a regular supply of water, and they do best in a very humid atmosphere. In addition, seeds need a stable temperature, a steady supply of light and protection from drafts.

If you do not wish to buy a complete kit, you can use a variety of containers in which to grow seeds. Aluminum pans or baking dishes, coffee cans and other household items can be put to use, so long as they have a depth of at least three inches. Remember that you will have to punch a number of small holes in the bottoms of such containers, to provide for drainage. Or you can buy small clay pots (by far the best container, I think, as long as you have only a few seeds).

The bottom of the pot, or whatever container you use, should be covered first with shards of crockery, and then with a loose layer of gravel or perlite. A small piece of crockery should be placed over each drainage hole. While you can prepare your own potting soil from its various components, I suggest you purchase a pre-mixed potting medium. Fill the pot with the mix, as you would if you were potting a mature plant.

After you have filled the container almost to its rim, water it thoroughly with a fine spray, or immerse the container to just below its rim in a pan or bucket of water. Allow the container to drain. Then sow the seeds. If you are using seeds that you have purchased from a garden supply center, the package should include instructions on how to sow the seeds (i.e. by placing them on the soil surface, covering them with a layer of soil mix, or placing them in slight depressions). If you are using seeds you have obtained elsewhere, I suggest you consult one of the several texts available on propagation, as different plants require different methods of seed placement.

Enclose the pot in a plastic bag or use sticks to prop a plastic sheet over the pot. Or, you can enclose other types of containers in a disused aquarium or other larger box. The idea is to keep the seeds in a humidity-rich atmosphere, while protecting them from fluctuations of temperature and from drafts. If none of these methods are practical, place the seed pot inside a larger pot that has been packed with peat moss or a mixture of sand and humus. You might even want to experiment by placing a pot on a small pebble tray.

Most seeds require a temperature during the day of between 70° to 75° to germinate. Again, exact requirements depend on the type of plant you are attempting to grow. Temperatures should be allowed to drop as low as 65° at night, as almost all types of seeds prefer this kind of temperature alternation.

Keep the growing mixture moist, but *do not* saturate it—just don't let it dry out. When leaves begin to appear, you can move the container into bright light, and you can remove the plastic or other protective covering. But *keep that soil moist*! Mist the plant daily. A very diluted dose of fertilizer can be given once very two weeks. When the seedling (or seedlings) is at least an inch high, you can then transplant it.

You can move them into a larger container, keeping several seedlings together. Or you can transplant a single seedling into a small clay pot—a pot large enough to hold the developing plant for at least six months. You can lift a seedling by grasping it very gently by a leaf. Try not to grasp it by its delicate stem. And *never* touch the roots—you will almost certainly damage them. Use a pencil or your finger to poke a depression in the soil surface of the new container. Lower the seedling into the depression, then gently brush soil around the roots until its lowest leaves are just above the soil surface. Water the seedling well as soon as you have transplanted it. Protect it from drafts. Keep it on a pebble tray or mist it regularly to provide adequate humidity—a seedling, even after it has been transplanted, requires more humidity than many mature plants. *Don't* overwater—don't let the soil become either dry or saturated: try to keep it moist. Once seedlings have been transplanted, give them the light conditions they require as mature plants; remember that different types of plants require differing amounts of light.

Seedlings must be carefully protected from the insect attacks, as they are much more vulnerable to a fatal infestation than a mature plant. Several pests seem to have a preference for tender young plants. Keep a close watch on your seedlings and on the soil for any signs of damage or disruption. Once seedlings have been attacked, it is almost impossible to save them. So you must act to prevent such problems. Keep the area around seedling pots or containers clean or free of debris. If you suspect trouble, transplant a seedling into another container with fresh soil. Don't treat a seedling with a dose of pesticide—if it looks very bad, you've probably already lost it. Pesticide applied to a badly damaged seedling won't help; pesticide applied to a healthy seedling may well kill it. And never, *never* pot a seedling in unsterilized soil.

Seedlings also suffer from damping-off disease (see page 80). I have been told that growing seeds in a medium other than potting soil greatly reduces the chances of a damping-off attack. Sphagnum moss or vermiculite are the substances most often mentioned as substitutes for a soil mix.

Fill a pot with the moss or vermiculite, as you would if you were using potting soil. Then immerse the containers almost to their rims in water to which a dose of fertilizer has been added (fertilizer packages will contain information on how much is needed according to the amount of water used). Moss and vermiculite contain few nutrients, while a potting mix (which will include moss and vermiculite as components) has a supply of several essential nutrients. So when you don't use a potting mix, you must compensate by adding a prepared fertilizer.

Place the seed, or seeds, on the surface of the material. If the seeds are rather large, place a thin layer of the material over them. Give these seeds the same treatment as you would any others, providing them with a humid environment, watering them from above with a fine spray, and allowing, at first, only bright, indirect light. Transplant them as you would any other seedlings.

SURGERY

Plant surgery involves removing infected or dying leaves or tissue with the use of a small, sharp knife, a razor or a pair of scissors. While surgery is an important technique, it is *not* a cure-all. It is only one step in the process of saving an ailing plant.

Don't react to indications of trouble by immediately whittling away at a drooping plant. Investigate the problem, determine the cause and establish a procedure for treatment. If your plant has soft and mushy tissue in the roots or, more rarely, along the stem, you will have to remove it.

Before operating, wash down the surface you intend to work on; also, thoroughly was your hands. Use a clean razor or knife to slice away diseased tissue. Don't hack and saw at the plant—make deliberate, even motions to cut the tissue cleanly away. After removing the diseased part, dust the exposed healthy tissue with a fungicide.

94

You can remove single leaves by pinching them off with your fingers as near as possible to the point where the leaf joins its stem. To do this, support the plant with one hand; apply pressure, but don't tug and rip.

A pair of small scissors can be used to trim away the browned ends of otherwise healthy leaves.

If you must remove an entire stem and several leaves, use a clean knife to cut away the stem just above the node (a node is the swollen growth on the plant stem from which stems and leaves issue).

When removing diseased tissue, discard the infected cuttings immediately. However, if a plant is failing and you are unable to save it, remember that you can take cuttings from any remaining healthy parts of the plant, and from these cuttings generate a new plant.

A cutting is any piece removed from the plant (most often a leaf or a stem) to be used for growing a new plant. Because cuttings lack roots at first, they must be treated with special care to insure that they receive sufficient moisture.

Cuttings should be grown in a very moist atmosphere, protected from the drying power of both the sun and strong drafts. You can best do this by keeping cuttings in some sort of protected environment. If you have a single cutting, you can place a clean glass jar over it. If you have several cuttings, you can place them in a pot, and rig a tent of plastic around the pot. Or, if you have a number of cuttings, you can use an aquarium or a terrarium, sealing the opening with a sheet of plastic.

Different plants are generated by different plant parts. For instance, African violets, echeveria, gloxinia, kalanchoe, peperomias and snake plant can all be propagated from a single leaf. Acalyphas, crown-of-throns, fuchsia, geraniums, gynuras and wandering jew are propagated from a stem cutting that does not include the stem's apex. However, many houseplants are best propagated by using cuttings of terminal pieces of stems, or, the end of the stems. It is a good idea to take a part of the stem having several leaves.

Leaf cuttings should be planted in a pot filled with sand, a combination of sand and peat moss, vermiculite or perlite. Plant the leaf so that its base, or the short stem to which it may be attached, is an inch below the surface of the soil. Whatever soil mix you use, be certain that it offers excellent drainage. And remember that if you have a single leaf cutting, you can invert a clean glass jar over it. The soil mix should be kept moist—but never saturated. Keep the cutting in a corner where it will receive plenty of indirect light, but will not be exposed to the direct rays of the sun.

A stem cutting should be at least four inches long. It is preferable to take a cutting that includes several nodes. It may be planted in sand, a combination of sand and peat moss, vermiculite or perlite. If you use vermiculite or perlite, fill the pot loosely—don't allow the material to become compacted.

Gently insert a stem cutting into a pot of perlite or vermiculite, until the cutting can stand erect on its own. As soon as you have positioned the cutting in place, mist with a fine spray. If you are planting in a mixture of sand and peat moss, prepare the container much as you would for transplanting a mature plant. You will need some sort of drainage material, and a piece of crockery to cover the drainage hole. Before you begin planting the cutting, dampen (but do not drench) the soil mix. Then take a pencil, and make a depression in the soil at least an inch deep. Remove all leaves from the bottom inch of the cutting. Gently set the stem in the hole, holding it upright as you lightly pack in soil mix around its base. After you have finished, give the cutting a long drink with a fine spray of water.

Throughout these procedures, everything must be kept clean. Use pasteurized soil mixes, clean pots and a sterile knife to take the cuttings. Whether you are using a jar, an old terrarium or an aquarium to provide a protected environment for the cutting, that container must be thoroughly scrubbed clean of all debris. Cuttings are extremely vulnerable to the attacks of pests and infections.

Very little ventilation will be required for the first week. The moist, protected environment of the container will encourage the healthy development of the cutting. You should, however, remove the covering twice a day to supply a light spray of water. After the first two weeks you can regularly remove the covering to begin conditioning the new plant to the normal atmosphere.

After three to four weeks, you can carefully dig the cutting up to see if roots have developed. If the new roots are now at least an inch or two long, you can transplant the cutting into a small pot and begin treating it as you would any young plant—giving it adequate supplies of water, light, foot and humidity, while keeping a close watch for any symptoms of trouble.

96

There are several commercial preparations available to encourage the growth of roots on cuttings. Available under such trade names as Rootone or Hormodin, these "rooting hormones" rapidly stimulate the growth of new roots. To apply, dip the bottom inch of a cutting in lukewarm water. Then, dip the bottom of the cutting in the powdered preparation. Make sure that the tip of the cutting is evenly—but not thickly—coated. Then plant it as you would any cutting.

You can also grow stem or leaf cuttings in a container of water, such as a jar or glass. In fact, this method may be a good way for you to clear out that collection of bottles you've had gathering dust on the windowsill. After you take a cutting, simply place it in a container of water at room temperature. Within two to three weeks you should see the first filaments of roots developing. When the roots have reached a length of from one to two inches, you can transplant the new plant as you would any other. While there are some experienced houseplant growers who believe this to be self-defeating in the long run (because, they say, the new roots will lack strength) I know several people who have had success after success using this method.

While such preparations are not miraculous in performance, they do often seem to lessen the time required to develop roots.

TERRARIUMS

A terrarium is a clear container holding a soil mix and a number of growing plants in a moist, protected environment. Terrariums have recently enjoyed great popularity. They are available in a wide range of sizes and styles. However, there are three basic types.

Covered terrariums have self-sustaining environments, made possible by the constant recycling of moisture in the container. The opening is sealed, and should be removed only for short periods of time.

Open terrariums are never sealed, and thus require more care.

Desert terrariums are composed of cacti and succulents and are never sealed.

Just as with house plants, you should buy only those terrariums having plants that can adapt to the amount of light in your home. Closed containers use humidity-loving plants. Such terrariums require several hours of bright, indirect light each day. If exposed to direct sunlight, the moisture cycle will be upset, the sun might burn leaves on the tender plants, and the plants might fail. Open containers have much the same light requirement. Desert terrariums, however, must have several hours of direct sunlight every day.

You can make a terrarium, with patience and attention to detail.

There are a number of glass containers that can double as terrariums, including fish tanks, brandy snifters, jars or large bottles. You will need a supply of sand, ground charcoal, potting mix and several plants.

The principle behind the terrarium is that plants produce vapor, and this liquid, combined with evaporation from the soil, is constantly recycled without much loss, providing a moist, balanced environment for plant growth.

Scrub the selected container thoroughly. Fill the bottom of the terrarium to the depth of about an inch with.sand or gravel. Mix ground charcoal into a small supply of your normal potting mix, and pour this mix into the terrarium until you have added another inch. The charcoal will absorb odors. Then pour in another two to three inches of a potting mix.

Plan the layout of your terrarium before you begin work, down to the smallest detail. Scoop small holes in the soil, and gently insert the plants, carefully patting down soil over the roots. You may add other decorative features, including shells, small rocks, bright pebbles or even small ceramic features. But be certain to *clean* each object thoroughly before you add it. Once introduced into the protected environment of a terrarium, an infection or a pest can rapidly devastate it.

Mold is a frequent problem for terrarium plants. It often occurs because of overwatering. The very humid environment inside the unit fosters the rapid spread of mold. When you discover a plant infected by mold, remove and destroy the entire plant. If several plants have been affected, remove them all. And if the infection seems especially virulent, remove *all* of the plants, retain only the healthiest, scrub the terrarium out and replant the unit. Before replanting the terrarium, you can lightly spray all of the plants with a fungicide dust. *Never* apply any kind of pesticide or fungicide directly to a terrarium—the sides of the units will be coated with a harmful residue. In addition, because there is considerably less ventilation inside a unit then is normally around a houseplant, the potency of any poison is greatly increased. You can, however, use a very light aerosol spray, *if* you can cover all the walls of the unit with sheets of paper that can be withdrawn after the application. After the spraying, leave a normally sealed container open for at least an hour to allow the vapors to dissipate.

Always use sterilized soil in your terrarium. Remember that unsterilized soil will certainly contain insect eggs and infections that will be stimulated into action by the humid atmosphere of a unit. Forethought is your best defense against insect problems in your unit.

I have heard of terrariums being infested by ants, aphids,

mealybugs, scale, thrips and white fly. These insects, as well as appropriate treatments for them, are described elsewhere in this book. When dealing with a houseplant, you have a fighting chance to save the plant and return it to health. But in a terrarium, an infestation can prove fatal almost overnight. The best way to rid a terrarium of insects is to completely clean it out, discarding infested plants, changing the soil, scrubbing out the unit and possibly dosing the replanted unit with a mild insecticide. While insects may find their way into an open terrarium, remember that the only way they can climb in a closed terrarium is because of your mistakes.

Plant diseases in a terrarium, as with all plants grown indoors, are caused by improper or inadequate growing conditions. Overwatering, or poor drainage, will result in crown, stem or root rot. Leaf loss may be caused by a deficiency of light or humidity. You can avoid such problems by carefully selecting plants for the unit according to their needs and your ability to supply them. Design your terrarium carefully, choose your plants well, and you can avoid most problems.

If the walls of the terrarium fog after the container has been sealed, you must allow greater circulation for the unit. Use a looser cover, or a cover with several small holes.

Watering procedures will vary from container to container. Some closed terrariums need additional water only once every few months. Open terrariums, however, need water much more often. No matter how often water must be given, add it sparingly. Give only so much water as the soil can absorb without appearing waterlogged. Remember, there is no exit for excess water in a terrarium—it stays to rot plant tissue and breed infections. Again, you can avoid overwatering by learning the preferences of the plants you intend to use. Try to stock your unit with plants compatible in their needs.

Terrariums constitute a unique form of gardening. While the needs of plants in an enclosed container are basically the same as other plants, there are differences in procedure. If you are interested in constructing your own miniature garden world, I suggest you consult any one of the several excellent books available on the subject.

ARTIFICIAL LIGHT GARDENING

If your rooms are but dimly illuminated by the sun, allowing you to grow only the hardiest of plants, you should consider the addition of artificial light. You can use fluorescent lamps either to supplement—or to entirely replace—the missing sunlight.

In addition to the wide variety of tubes that can be adapted for "light" gardening, there are now available such units as the "Plant-Light," "Plant-Gro" or "Gro-Lux," which have been manufactured especially for indoor gardening. I recommend the use of such lighting units because they have been specifically designed with plant needs in mind. While you can rig a lighting system yourself, composed of incandescent and fluorescent lamps, you take the chance of getting the balance wrong and failing to supply your plants with the light they need. In addition, remember that incandescent lamps often project heat intense enough to burn the tissue of plants placed too close to them.

You will have to expose your plants to artificial light for a much longer period than you would have to keep them in sunlight, as even the brightest of indoor units is far weaker than the sun. This of course means a slightly larger utility bill—but, if this is the only way you can grow full, healthy plants in your home, you may consider it a worthwhile expenditure.

Colorless foliage, weak stems and shriveled blooms occuring on plants grown under lights indicate that the light is insufficient. Remember that, just as different plants require differing amounts of sunlight, certain varieties will require differing amounts of artificial light. There is now quite a bit of literature available on indoor light gardening, and I recommend that you consult it for specific recommendations on establishing a "light" garden.

I especially like the use of artificial lights because they can be used in so many ways. You can supplement the light in your rooms. You can grow some of your plants entirely under light units. Or you can use one unit just for flowering certain plants, or for supplying just the amount of light seedlings need to grow. In addition, such units can be quite attractive, brightening up otherwise dull corners or parts of rooms.

When you buy or build such a unit, keep in mind the normal requirements of your plants. Establish the unit in a location generally protected from drafts, away from heat outlets and frequently used doors. If, for some reason, you cannot find such a location in the space you have available, you can establish an indoor light garden inside an aquarium or some other large glass case.

You can now purchase entire light gardens, which include a balanced lighting system and several shelves to hold plants. Some units are as large as carts and, like carts, are on wheels so that they can be easily moved about. There are also a variety of plants available for building a unit yourself. One of the most ingenious ideas I have heard calls for placing the plants on a pebble tray, under the lights, thus combining an adequate supply of humidity with a balanced amount of light. As with all aspects of growing houseplants, your imagination is one of the most important tools you have.

You can secure information about "light" gardening not only from books, but from the manufacturers of specific units, from the Extension service of the nearest agricultural college and from horticultural societies.

Last Word

I wrote **The Plant Doctor** because I personally needed such a book about ailing house plants for some time. I too had my share of sick house plants, and have spent many desperate hours thumbing through book after book in search for an elusive remedy. Unfortunately, the more I thumbed, the faster my poor plants wilted and withered. That's because most plant books are only written about *well* plants, and hardy utter a word about ill plants. Which is fine, until you have a plant fall ill.

I often had the uncomfortable feeling that no one else ever lost a house plant, and that I was doing something wrong that no one else did. Judging by the glowing optimism of many plant books, it seemed plausible that everyone else was enjoying rows of healthy, eternally-growing house plants while I was battling the most recent in a succession of white fly attacks or mold growths. But the more I talked to other indoor gardeners, the more I realized how false that impression was, and how great was the need for a book that focused on the problems of ailing house plants as opposed to only healthy ones.

After researching for **The Plant Doctor**, I realized how badly I underestimated the number and variety of possible ills, as well as the frequency with which they occur. But the single most important thing I learned—and I freely pass it on as helpful advice—is that the majority of plant problems are caused by us, the plant owners, and not by chance, bad luck or Mother Nature. We set the stage for the trouble to follow by giving a plant too much or too little water, the wrong amount of sunlight or any number of other simple, common but oftimes fatal mistakes.

But if we are the cause for such problems, we can also provide the remedy. Almost all plant problems can be corrected or cured rapidly and permanently, if we are willing to take the time and trouble.

So if this book helps you save even one suffering plant, it will have served its purpose. I hope that it will also encourage a realistic, responsible attitude towards plant care. In conclusion, I just want to say that we all have a responsibility to our environment—be it a small farm in the country or the 23rd floor of a center city condominium—and once we have assumed dominance over any area of natural life, even if it is only a small, insignificant house plant, we have a responsibility to use that power wisely and sparingly.

PLANT RESOURCES

SEEDS

Alberts and Merkel Brothers, Inc.　　　　*tropical plants,*
Boynton Beach, Florida 33435　　　　　　　　　　*orchids*

Burgess Seed and Plant Company　　　*seeds, and plants*
P.O. Box 218, Galesburg, Michigan 49053

W. A. Burpee Company　　　　　　　　*annual, biennial*
　　　　　　　　　　　　　　　　　and perennial seeds

Farmer Seed and Nursery Company
Fairbault, Minnesota 55021

Herbst Brothers, Seedsmen
1000 North Main Street, Brewster, New York 10905

D. Landreth Seed Company
2700 Wilmarco Avenue, Baltimore, Maryland 21223

L.L. Olds Seed Company
Box 1068, 2901 Packers Avenue, Madison Wisconsin 53701

R.H. Shumway, Seedsman,
628 Cedar Street, Rockford, Illinois 61101

Carino Nurseries　　　　　　　　　　　　　*seedlings*
Box 538, Indiana, Pennsylvania 15701

Silver Falls Nursery　　　　　　　　　　　*seedlings*
Star Route, Box 5, Silverton, Oregon 97381

IN CANADA

Chipman Chemical Limited　　*selection of fungicides,*
Hamilton, Ontario　　　　　　　　　　　*insecticides*

GTE Sylvania Canada, Limited　*line of indoor lighting*
8750 Cote de Liesse Road, Montreal,　*products, incl. lamps*
Quebec H4T 1H3

Horican Sales Company　　　　　　　　　*hand tools*
P.O. Box 10, Station "Z"
Toronto, Ontario M5N Z2J

National Garden Supply of Canada, Limited   *complete line of*
150 Duke street, Bowmanville, Ontario   *gardening supplies*

United Co-Operatives of Ontario   *fertilizers, fungicides,*
2549 Weston Road, Weston, Ontario   *insecticides, seeds, tools*

PLANT SOCIETIES

There are a number of plant societies now active in the United States.
Many of them maintain excellent libraries, and some of them publish
newsletters or magazines. And all of them should be able to answer
your questions or direct you to someone who can. If you are serious
about building a plant collection, I suggest you get in touch with a
society. You might also enjoy the pleasure of exchanging
information, soil recipes and tips on plant care with people as
interested in plants as you are.

African Violet Society of America   *Publishes the*
P.O. Box 1326, Knoxville, Tennessee 37901**African Violet Magazine**

American Fern Society   *Publishes the*
415 South Pleasant Street,   **American Fern Journal**
Amherst, Massachusetts 01002

American Plant Life Society   *Publish*
Box 150, La Jolla, California 92037   **Plant Life**

Cactus and Succulent Journal
132 West Union Street, Pasadena, California 91101

Massachusetts Horticultural Society   *Publishes a*
300 Massachusetts Avenue   *monthly magazine*
Boston, Massachusetts 02115   **Horticulture**

Pennsylvania Horticultural Society   *Publishes a*
325 Walnut Street   *bimonthly magazine,*
Philadelphia, Pennsylvania 19106   **The Green Scene**

SUPPLIERS OF INDOOR LIGHTING EQUIPMENT INCLUDE:

Armstrong Associates, Inc.
Box 127 BK, Basking Ridge, New Jersey 07920

Craft House Manufacturing Company
Wilson, New York 10706

Floralite Company
4124 East Oakwood Road, Oak Creek, Wisconsin 53221

Lifelite Incorporated
1025 Shary Circle, Concord, California 94520

Radar Fluorescent Company
63 15th Street, Brookly, New York

Rapid Lite
245 South Broadway, Yonkers, New York 10705

Shoplite Company
566 J Franklin Avenue, Nutley, New Jersey 07110

Tube Craft, Inc.
1311 W. 80th Street, Cleveland, Ohio 44102

BIBLIOGRAPHY

There are scores of house plant books currently available, and many more plant books now out of print but still to be found on library shelves. I have not attempted a survey of the field. Instead, I have limited this bibliography to a list of the books *I* found to be instructive during my research.

Ballard, Ernesta D.: **Growing Plants Indoors: A Garden in Your House.** *New York, Barnes and Noble, 1973.*
Crockett, James: **Flowering House Plants.** *(Encyclopedia of Gardening Series), New York, Time-Life Books, 1971.*
   Foliage House Plants. *New York, Time-Life Books, 1972.*
Cruso, Thalasso: **Making Things Grow: A Practical Guide to Indoor Gardening.** *New York, Knopf, 1969.*
Douglas, James Sholto: **Beginners Guide to Hydroponics.** *New York, Drake Publishers, 1972.*
   Gardening *without* soil is a recent developement. Surprisingly, it's not difficult, it requires little space, and you get results more rapidly than with soil. This is a clear, complete guide to a fascinating field.
Dworkin, Florence and Dworkin, Stanley: **Apartment Gardener.** *New York, New American Library, 1974.*

One of the best paperback plant books on the market, and *not* just for apartment gardeners. Anyone with house plants should find it instructive.

Faust, Joan Lee: **The New York Times Book of House Plants.** *New York, Quadrangle, 1973.*

Fitch, Charles Marden: **The Complete Book of Houseplants.** *New York, Hawthorn Books, 1972.*

Both the Times book and the Fitch book are comprehensive, detailed volumes. I recommend either book as the foundation of your house plant library.

Free, Montague: **Plant Propagation in Pictures.** *Garden City, Doubleday, 1957.*

"How to increase the number of plants in your home and garden by division, grafting, layering, cuttings, bulbs and tubers, sowing seeds and spores". (from the cover). There are several books covering this subject—I prefer Free's volume.

Haring, Elda: **Complete Book of Growing Plants from Seed.** *New York, Hawthorn, 1967.*

Jenkins, Dorothy H.: **Encyclopedia of House Plants.** *New York, Bantam, 1974.*

Excellent introductory text, available in paperback.

Kranz, Frederick H. and Jacqueline L.: **Gardening Indoors Under Lights.** *New York, Viking, 1971.*

Probably the best book available on gardening under artificial light.

Prenis, John: **Herb Grower's Guide.** *Philadelphia, Running Press, 1974.*

Herbs are easily grown, and many varieties can become additions as spices to your meals. Can you say as much for a begonia? An informative, practical guidebook that will turn you into a herb-growing expert.

Riker, Tom and Rottenberg, Harvey: **The Gardener's Catalog.** *New York, William Morrow, 1974.*

An ample collection of information, gadgets, sources of supplies, charts, recommendations and everything else about gardening. The "Whole Earth" of plants?

Sunset Editors: **How to Grow House Plants.** *California, Lane, 1968.*

Taylor, Norman (ed.): **Taylor's Encyclopedia of Gardening.** *Boston, Houghton Mifflin, 1961.*

1300 pages covering *every* aspect of gardening. Its price ($17.50) makes it a luxury, but there really isn't anything quite like it. And it's large enough to make a plant stand when you're not happily thumbing through it.

Westcott, Cynthia: **The Gardener's Bug Book.** *Garden City, Doubleday, 1973.*

Everything Cynthia Westcott writes is full of information and practical sense. This volume is the single most thorough reference volume on garden pests. Descriptions, plants affected and treatments are given for every but harmful to green life. Comprehensive, authoritative, a marvel of research. . . if you're growing a number of plants, indoors or out, you should add this book to your library.

INDEX

108